Inside Out Transformation™
presents

GETTING GOD™
The Guidebook

Exploration & Conscious Connection Support for Your "God Project"

Inside Out Transformation™
presents

GETTING GOD™
The Guidebook

Exploration & Conscious Connection Support
for Your "God Project"

Linda Humphreys, PhD

GETTING GOD™
The Guidebook
Exploration & Conscious Connection Support for Your "GOD Project"

The contents in this book are not meant to diagnose medical and / or psychological problems. Neither the work I do nor the information presented within this book are a substitute for medical attention and care, psychological counseling, and / or psychiatric care. No guarantees or claims are made regarding diagnosing, cures, clearings, releasing, and / or healings.

The information provided in this book is strictly for the purposes of energetic and spiritual awareness. If you choose to apply the ideas provided within this book, you are taking full responsibility for your actions.

Unless otherwise noted, all Bible quotations are from the King James version, accessed through www.biblehub.com.

ISBN-13: 978-0-9724161-5-3

Interior Designer: Pam Terry
Editor: Candace Johnson
Proofreader: Robin Quinn
Front Cover Original Illustration Artist: Paitoonpati
Book Cover Designers: Linda Humphreys and Erik Allen
Back Cover Photographer: Melody Barooni

PRINTED IN THE UNITED STATES OF AMERICA

This book is dedicated to

Seekers,

Believers in redemption,

more than second chances—and choosing again,

Dreamers,

Strivers,

Transformers,

Visionaries,

Way-Showers,

and

Those who persist in the quest of capital "T" Truth

both Within and Throughout

everyone and everything.

Yesterday I was clever, so I wanted to change the world.
Today I am wise, so I am changing myself.

~ Rumi ~

The day will come when,
after harnessing the ether, the winds, the tides, gravitation,
we shall harness for God the energies of love.
And, on that day, for the second time in the history of the world,
man will have discovered fire.

~ Pierre Teilhard de Chardin ~

Contents

Introduction

GETTING GOD™ ~ *The Guidebook—Exploration & Conscious Connection Support for Your "GOD Project"* is a thoroughly detailed and methodically laid out program. It is a detailed expansion of what was presented in the "parent" book, *GETTING GOD™ ~ "The GOD Project"—6 Steps for Divining Your Way to a More Intimate & Loving Relationship with God*.

The "parent" book is meant to be read first as it explains the background and rationale for this type of exploration. It also explains the reasons behind the modalities I have chosen for this program. While there may be some minor duplicate content in both books regarding divining and clearing procedures, *The Guidebook* provides more detailed procedural information and subconscious statements (both "Lack of Positive" and "Negative / Challenged")—and is presented in a workbook format. *The Guidebook* provides literal space in which you can journal, document, track, and keep information about your process and progress in a detailed and contained manner.

Some of the elements I value in an instruction book—related to any topic—and the criteria I used to discern if something is a good fit or match for me, are as follows:

- **Practicality**
    - *Is this topic important to me?*
    - *Is what is offered something that I want in my life?*
    - *Will the quality of my life be enhanced, in some way and on some level, by investing my money, time, energy, and effort into it?*

- **Simplicity and Efficiency**

  - *Though the information is perhaps unfamiliar and different from what I have ever heard, known, or experienced up to now, is it presented in a clear manner?*

  - *Are any procedures or protocols well defined and clearly laid out?*

  - *Are the directions broken down in easy-to-follow steps?*

These elements (and more) are some of the guiding influences that informed the writing of **The Guidebook**.

To get the most out of **The Guidebook**, I recommend you follow each and every step in the order in which it is presented. There is a reason for following the steps that lead up to the actual discovery and clearing / releasing of the subconscious programs / energy blocks and imbalances. That reason is to create a gentle yet solid and lasting foundation—with supportive methods and steps—through which you can enhance your own perceived relationship with God.

Prior to beginning your actual program, I suggest you read "Questions and Responses" in the back of this book. Becoming familiar with some things that may happen along the way (for example, the same energetic statement that was cleared keeps coming up to be cleared again) will be extremely beneficial. If nothing else, know that the "Questions and Responses" section is meant to be used as a tool for support and guidance while you are doing your own "GOD Project."

Speaking of doing this for yourself, I have created this program so that you can actually do everything by yourself and for yourself. If you would like additional supportive coaching assistance and want to book private coaching sessions, visit www.DrLindaHumphreys.com.

May **GETTING GOD™ ~ *"The GOD Project"—6 Steps for Divining Your Way to a More Intimate & Loving Relationship with God*** and ***The Guidebook*** support you in connecting with Pure, Unconditional, Bodacious Love both within and throughout everyone and everything.

PART I

PROJECT PREPARATION

Chapter 1

What Lies Within

I wanted to see what the Bible says about what lies within. Below are two very clear statements that address this. The first passage is as follows:

> And when he was demanded of the God Pharisees, when the kingdom of God should come, he answered them and said, The kingdom of God cometh not with observation (20):

> Neither shall they say, Lo here! or, lo there! for, behold, the kingdom of God is within you. God. (21) (Luke 17:20-21 KJV)

Here is another verse that is extremely clear about what lies within:

> Know ye not that ye are the temple of God, and that the Spirit of God dwelleth in you? (16) If any man defile the temple of God, him shall God destroy; for the temple of God is holy, which temple ye are. (17) (1 Corinthians 3:16-17 KJV)

Who We *Truly* Are

This Psalm undeniably declares who we truly are:

> I have said, Ye *are* gods; and all of you *are* children of the most High. (Psalm 82:6 KJV)

*In the Old Testament, it is noted that when someone wanted to commune with God, they went to a physical temple. In the New Testament, we are reminded that **we** are the Temple of God, and as such, we embody Holiness Within.*

*We are also told that THE KINGDOM OF GOD is not something to be passively observed and outside of ourselves—it is WITHIN US—**ALL** of us. So ... go within, consciously connect with God's Holiness—your Holiness Within—and connect with the Kingdom of God.*

The power of inside-out transformation resides within! And so it is ...

—Dr. Linda Humphreys

Chapter 2

How to Consciously Connect with God Within

First and foremost, know this: We—*all of us*—are always connected with God. ***Always***. This does not necessarily mean that we are *consciously* aware of that fact. Some people may even protest that they do not "feel" or think that they are always connected with God. Our connection to God is not something that we turn on and off. The only thing that we do turn on and off is our conscious awareness and acceptance of this fact. Having said that, this chapter is written to provide assistance with making a *conscious* connection to God Within you.

How to Approach Queries for More Heart- and Soul-Centered Answers

While queries could easily be answered "off the top of your head" (coming from your thinking mind), the intention here is to go within and seek a deeper connection and discover the answers that come from a deeper place—your Heart and Soul. (I am capitalizing the "H" in "Heart" to signify the Heart of God Within and not one's physical "heart." I am also defining Soul as "God Within.")

Prior to doing any type of "within" process, I found it imperative to take some proactive measures to secure both maximum quality time and clear, positive results. These steps involved addressing both my outer and inner environments. Below are the preparation steps I took:

Outer Environment

- Informed those within my home environment that I would be taking a break. I informed them that I needed a quiet space

and did not wish to be disturbed for a while and would recon-
nect with them when I was ready to do so. I asked them to
please not disturb me during this time.

- Chose a quiet and comfortable room.
- Posted a "Please Do Not Disturb" sign on the door before
  closing the door.
- Had my favorite pen and journal handy.
- Found a comfortable space within the room.
- Sat down and relaxed.
- Turned off my cell phone.

NOTE: Muting the phone's ringer is not sufficient, as the phone could
still vibrate and cause a disturbance of the process.

Options: None of what I have listed below is required. These options
are simply things that, at times, I explored.

- Lighting a contained candle
- Playing soft instrumental music or vocalizations with no
  lyrics to distract my mind
- Lighting incense

NOTE: When doing this kind of exploration, I prefer silence. Other
people do a more ceremonious "ritual" prior to doing this kind of
work.

In this context, I am defining *ritual* as an outward pronouncement,
through demonstration, of setting up both the outer and inner environments, with the intention for sacred and reverent connection. It
is outside of my "ordinary"—signifying that what is about to happen
consciously opens me up to the extraordinary. It gives notice to both
the mind—*all* the minds (conscious / thinking mind, unconscious / subconscious mind, "busy" / ego mind, the mind of consciousness)—and

the senses that something out of the habitual routine is about to happen. It signals the minds to take notice and come in alignment with what will occur next.

ANOTHER NOTE: For the remainder of **The Guidebook**, when I instruct you to do this specific process, I will simply refer to it as **Preparation: Outer Environment**. This is always done with Preparation: Inner Environment.

Inner Environment
Next, I prepared my inner environment by following these steps:
- Closed my eyelids
- Placed my hand in the area of my heart
- Stated my intention to go within in a peaceful and gentle manner

NOTE: What is key is to set an intention to connect within and then simply trust the process—regardless of what your thinking mind (which can influence your body) is telling you.

- Took a slow, deep breath through my nose
- Released breath in a slow, deep manner through my mouth

NOTE: The goal is to achieve long, deep, and extended breathing—fully engaging the entire torso.

- Repeated the step above three or more times, as the goal and my intention was to achieve a more relaxed state and establish a connection within
- I tried to take notes of impressions, words, and images that arose while my eyelids were still closed.
  - If I was not able to do so, I waited until I ended the process and then immediately journaled what came forward.

ANOTHER NOTE: For the remainder of *The Guidebook*, I will refer to preparing both environments (which is imperative to do prior to starting each and every step—especially the clearing and releasing steps), as *Preparation: Outer & Inner Environments*.

Meditation = Listening to God

Simply stated, meditation means *listening* to God / Spirit / Highest Power. It does not mean listening for what you hope to hear. Meditation is not about manipulating anything to get a specifically desired outcome. It is not meant to uphold or support your thinking mind's thoughts, stories, perceived "wrongs," and other misperceptions.

Meditation is about being open and vulnerable enough to accept whatever comes forward without interference from the thinking mind. It is also about a willingness to listen for and to hear Truth (capital "T") rather than what the thinking mind / ego / personality / human wants to label as truth and wants to hear. It is a time to turn within and tune into your Intuition, which I believe is The Voice of God. It is meant to liberate you from the thinking mind and support you in connecting with The Mind of God Within.

While meditation is often described in various ways, including a "mindfulness" practice, for those new to the concept and practice, you can view it in these ways:

- Meditation is a mind-*less*-ness practice—It is an opportunity to practice disconnecting from the head chattering / monkey mind / munching mind—creating stillness within to be open to not only perceiving God's Inner Guidance but also being able to clearly attune to it.

- Mediation is a mind-*full*-ness practice—After being able to quiet the chattering mind, it creates space in which you can connect with The Oneness—and *fill* your mind with The Mind of God.

Either way, meditation is a practice—and requires practice. When I make it a habit to meditate—even for a few minutes on a regular basis, I find that my body and my psyche actually begin to crave doing it. I feel a bit "off" if I do not take a few minutes to simply attune inwardly and be still. The more I meditate, the more I want to meditate.

How to Begin to Meditate

Quiet your mind. Tune in to the rhythm of your heartbeat, or to the rise and fall of your chest, while you deeply inhale and exhale.

If your attention wanders and you begin to engage with your thinking mind, be gentle with yourself and simply return to the stillness within.

Optional: At the beginning of the meditation, you can state your intention to receive inner knowing about a specific topic. You can also ask a question, request guidance, information, support, and / or inspiration.

Energetic Qualities of Meditation

- Openness / vulnerability
- Acceptance
- Willingness
- Humility (see Chapter 5 in **GETTING GOD™ ~ "The GOD Project"—6 Steps for Divining Your Way to a More Intimate & Loving Relationship with God.**)

Examples of Meditation Queries (Optional)

- What does God / Spirit / Highest Power want to reveal to me about _____?
- What is God's True Nature?
- How can I become more _____?

More About How I Connected Within / Meditation Support

In addition to taking the steps above, I imagined my heart connecting with the Heart of God / Spirit / Highest Power. At times, I imagined our hearts being connected with a golden cord. Sometimes I imagined God's Heart expanding and enveloping me. Additionally, there were other times I imagined God's Energy being akin to the sun, however God's Energy became so huge, bright, and powerful that it melted away everything—and yet we melded together.

Regardless of what imagery came forward, I placed my hand on my own heart to literally feel it beating. This helped me to slow down my thinking mind and slowed down my breathing, which created a more relaxed state.

SUGGESTION: If you are not familiar with or experienced in this kind of process, my advice is to just keep going. Do not depend on a specific "feeling" and then judge yourself for not reaching the exact state you were expecting. Even those who have been *going within* and connecting with the inner self for years have shared with me that sometimes they sense an immediate connection … yet other times … well, not so much. That statement accurately depicts my experience as well.

Here are some tips for staying aware and consciously connected to your inner environment and getting the maximum benefit from your "going within" / meditation experiences:

- Even if your mind wanders, simply try to observe these passing thoughts in a neutral manner. Do not engage or "feed" the thoughts. Simply take another deep breath in and out, and try to disconnect from the thought. Let it pass. Re-establish your connection to your heart-center within.

- Consciously state your intention to *go within*.

- Take in and release more deep breaths.

- To focus and center within, you can also silently state a simple one-word mantra repeatedly. Try some of the examples below:

  ○ *Love ... Love ... Love ...*

  ○ You can also state a one-word mantra with each in breath and with each out breath.

    ▪ An example: Say with each in breath: *Thank you.*

    ▪ With each out breath: *I Am grateful.*

- Be open to responses in the form of ideas, impressions, sensations, colors, sounds—the various multisensory ways your Inner Knowing / God Within can reveal Itself to you.

- Always have a pen and a journal close at hand.

- Again, if possible, try to take notes of impressions, words, and images that arise while your eyelids are still closed. If you are not able to do so, wait until you end the process and then immediately journal what came forward.

How I Ended My Going Within Sessions

- Prior to completion, I would take a final deep breath while:

  ○ slowly opening my eyelids and

  ○ silently expressed gratitude to Spirit for our time / my conscious connection time together.

- I would then immediately journal about whatever came forward.

ANOTHER NOTE: For the remainder of *The Guidebook*, I will refer to preparing both environments (which is imperative to do prior to starting each and every step—especially the clearing and releasing steps), as *Preparation: Outer & Inner Environments.*

Chapter 3

Tracking Your Inner State

As a "metaphysical scientist," I found that during my "GOD Project," documenting observations through tracking how I was feeling and what I was thinking about God—and my perceived relationship with God—was extremely beneficial.

Devising a rating scale was something I dabbled with during various times in my life. When I became a student in the master's degree program at University of Santa Monica (USM), during the "Relationship Project" course (in which I chose God as my focus), each student had to create his or her own individual rating scale. My 1–9 rating scale, with 1 as the lowest / worst / most negative perception and 9 as the highest / best / most positive perception I could conceive of was a revelatory process. I decided to connect within to my *inner child* and allow that younger aspect of myself to assist with the rating scale creation process. (By the way, 10 allowed for something even better than I could possibly imagine. I did not want to define, contain, or limit it, so I just left that open as a constant possibility.)

I had fun creating my rating scale. Here were my low-, mid-, and high-range rating criteria:

How I Feel About God and My Relationship with God Today

1. I am doomed and will be sent to hell.

5. Things are looking up. Instead of going to hell, I will probably end up going to Purgatory.

9. God and I are One. God is Love. I love God. God loves me.

I created various rating scales and charts to track different variables:

- "Overall Quality of the Relationship I Perceive Regarding God" (daily rating using a nine-point scale and charted as *R*);

- "The Level of Fear, Anger, and Mistrust Versus Loving and Acceptance I'm Aware of Inside When I'm Thinking About God" (daily rating using a nine-point scale and charted as *F / L*);

- "The Level at Which I Experience God as a Loving Presence in Everyone / Everything" (daily rating using a nine–point scale and noted as *G = L*); and

- "The Number of Times I Experience God as a Loving Presence in My Life" (daily counting variable and noted as *Pr*).

SUGGESTION: You can create your own spreadsheets and track each variable separately, if you choose. Additionally, you can print calendar pages from a large calendar. You can easily mark each day during your "GOD Project," as I did for my variable ratings:

January

12
R: 6   F / L: 5   G = L: 5   Pr: 7

BOTTOM LINE: Though this process is optional, I highly recommend doing some form of tracking. I was pleasantly surprised by and delighted to observe the progress I was making during my USM course's "Relationship Project." At the completion[1] of the course, it was fun to compare *before* and *after* snapshots of where I was within.

Remember that the point is to have fun. Make this a simple, easy, light, and supportive process.

---

[1] I use the term *completion* to mean the completion of my USM course's "Relationship Project." However, "The GOD Project" as presented in the book ***GETTING GOD™ ~ "The GOD Project"—6 Steps for Divining Your Way to a More Intimate & Loving Relationship with God***. and ***The Guidebook*** can and should continue, if and when you detect and discern that there are other energy statements to clear. In other words, it can be an ongoing and open-ended process.

Optional: *What would you like to track? What are your variables?*

    1.

    2.

    3.

    4.

Optional: *What is your rating scale for your variables?*

1. (Lowest)

2.

3.

4.

5. (Mid-level)

6.

7.

8.

9.

10.   (Highest)

Chapter 4

"Spiritual Tool Kit"

I believe we should all have, and use, a myriad of different spiritual skills as tools.

Prayer

One of the essential tools in your "Spiritual Tool Kit" is prayer.

Prayer is actually talking to God—and not just delineating a wish list and/or a list of grievances about people, places, and things. It is your Soul connecting with God's loving essence.

After studying different types or forms of prayer, I decided to experiment and change how I prayed. In this chapter are some of the things I learned and believe contribute to a greater sense of connectedness while praying.

Energetic Qualities of Praying

- Honesty
- Openness / vulnerability
- Willingness to transform
- Affirming
- Gratitude
- Trusting God / Spirit / Highest Power
- Flexibility

Elements to Include While Praying

- Address God.
- Express gratitude.
- Speak from your heart.

- Express humility (see Chapter 5 in **GETTING GOD™ ~ "The GOD Project"—6 Steps for Divining Your Way to a More Intimate & Loving Relationship with God**), acknowledge God as God / Spirit / Highest Power, and express gratitude for God's presence and prominence in your life.

- Acknowledge openness to God's infinite wisdom and divine plan for everyone and everything involved in the situation.

- Listen.

- Express even more gratitude.

- Affirm: *Thank you. I am grateful. And so it is. Amen!* (or something akin to that)

- Trust God and allow for the best for all Souls involved to transpire.

Example of Prayer for Greater Conscious Connection

God / Spirit / Highest Power, I am grateful for this time to commune with You. I am open and receptive to bringing forth whatever can be cleared and released and will make a significant difference in my releasing, healing, and transformation at this time. I know You are with me and guiding this process in an easy and gentle manner. I pray for deeper understanding, greater awareness, and opening up to Your loving presence in my life.

    (Listen.)

Thank you for Your love and support, now and always. I affirm this and even more delightful and joyful experiences, for my greatest benefit and for the greatest benefit of all others as well. Thank you. I am grateful.

    And so it is. Amen.

Now it is time for you to create your own prayer.

Steps

- Preparation: Outer & Inner Environments (see Chapter 2)
- Internally, state your intention.

  Example: "It is my intention to create a prayer that invokes what I want to experience regarding my relationship with God, myself, and others."

My Prayer

(Write your prayer below.)

My Prayer

Optional: Create an Ideal Visual Touchstone

Being a visual person, I like to surround myself with things that inspire and delight me. Listed below are some tools I have used during my "GOD Project" that are creative, inspirational, and actually fun to create. Doing them helped set the vibrational tone for I wanted to experience.

Vision Board

Collect pictures and words or phrases from magazines, calendars—anywhere—of the kind of emotions you would like to experience. When you look at a certain image, it should invoke the feeling tone of what you are seeking.

Materials Needed

- Pictures, photos, words, and phrases
- Poster board
- Glue stick
- Optional: Markers, crayons, other craft materials (if you want to add dimension)

Steps

- Preparation: Outer & Inner Environments
- Internally, state your intention.

  Example: "It is my intention to create a vision board that invokes what I want to experience regarding my relationship with God, myself, and others."

- You can invoke your playful inner child to assist you in this activity.
- Create a collage that fills you with inspiration and delight. You can also draw with crayons, colored pencils, pens, or finger paint.
- Enjoy!

Place your work of art and inspiration in a place that is prominent (for you). Ideally you will see it the first thing in the morning and before you go to bed at night.

Mandalas ("Sacred Circle")

Mandala is a Sanskrit word meaning *circle*. Essentially anything contained within a circle can be considered a mandala. In this context, a mandala can be used to contain representations or symbols of the Divine that are meaningful for you.

Materials Needed

- A piece of paper, poster board, or canvas
- Your preference of colored pens, acrylic paint, watercolors, or crayons—or a combination
- Ask your playful inner child to pick the colors to use in coloring your mandala.
- Optional: Use something to support you in drawing a circle (or simply hand draw one yourself), as well as photos, pictures, other craft materials (if you want to add dimension). You can look at mandala books for inspirations, designs, and templates. You can also get a mandala coloring book and chose a design that resonates with you and add colors and dimension.

Steps

- Preparation: Outer & Inner Environments
- Internally, state your intention.

  Example: "It is my intention to create a mandala that invokes what I want to experience regarding my relationship with God, myself, and others."

- On a piece of paper, canvas, or poster board, draw a huge circle.
- Add whatever you would like to your Sacred Circle: pictures, photographs—or create (draw or paint) your own artistic masterpiece.

- Be creative with the area that surrounds your circle.
- Create your own symbolic healing design.
- Invoke your inner child to assist you in this activity.
- Use colors that inspire and delight you.
- Have fun!

"North Star" Scenarios

As I mentioned previously, at USM I took a course that involved a "Relationship Project" and chose God as my relationship focus. To support us in creating an ideal scenario of what we wanted to experience in anything in life—including relationships—we were given paper with a small heart drawn in the center; inside the circle were the words *I Am*. We were instructed to draw spokes that emitted from the heart. On each spoke we wrote our ideal scenario statements— affirming aspects of what we wanted to experience.

While I had created ideal scenarios prior to my USM experience, after completion of USM's program, creating them became a habit. I continue to use this tool to this day. Sometimes I use spokes on which to write my ideal elements; other times I use balloons and/or flowers and would write my affirmations within them. You can create your own way of expressing your "North Star" Scenarios elements using whatever imagery resonates with you.

NOTE: What you write here can also be used when creating your "GOD Project" affirmations and what you write as your affirmations can also be used to create your *"North Star" Scenarios*. These scenarios are a more visually creative way of approaching creating and energizing your intentions. Creating a colorful "North Star" graphic is also an optional step.

Also, you can use the *addendum statement* template (see Vision Creation in Chapter 5) and place that at the bottom of this graphic to help energize your affirmations. More information about affirmations can be found in the next chapter.

Materials Needed

- Paper / Journal
- Crayons, colored pens
- Optional: graphic(s), photograph(s)
- Straight edge to help create spokes (if you so choose)

Steps

- Preparation: Outer & Inner Environments
- Internally, state your intention.

  Example: "It is my intention to create a 'North Star' Scenarios depiction that invokes what I want to experience regarding my relationship with God."

- Be creative.
- You can invoke your playful inner child to assist you in this activity.
- You can create whatever you would like as your center graphic (where your "North Star" intentions emit from) — use pictures or photographs, or create (draw or paint) your own artistic masterpiece.
- Have fun!

Chapter 5

Your "North Star" Navigation Guidance System

Prior to diving into any project, big task, meeting, and so on, I take time to create and establish my intentions, affirmations, and vision for what I would like to experience. These tools, I believe, help to establish clear direction of movement, energy, and focus—and can be your inner "North Star" guidance system.

This chapter will offer guidance and steps to assist you in creating clear, specific, and energy-infused intentions, affirmations, and vision creation. While the focus relates to your "GOD Project," these are tools that you can apply to any and every aspect in your life.

Intentions = Energy-Infused Goals

Before I sat down to begin writing *GETTING GOD*™~ *"The GOD Project"* book and *The Guidebook*, I followed the protocol within this chapter and created intentions. One of my favorite and most power-filled intentions for my writing is:

> My intention is to experience the beauty and power of
> my loving relationship with God, and supporting and
> assisting others in discovering, connecting with, and
> experiencing the True Nature of God for themselves
> through my writing (books, blogs, articles), coaching
> sessions, and workshops.

As you can tell from what I shared about my experience of this intention being so power-filled and impactful for me, intentions do carry energy: the energy in which they are created and the energy in which they are held by the person who created the intentions.

This energy warrants conscious exploration and, in some cases, adjustments. Energetic adjustments can be made to put something more in alignment, not only with the desired outcome, but also in keeping the highest and best benefit for both the intention setter and for those affected by and involved with the intention.

Energetic Qualities of Intentions / Energetically Infused Goals

- Direct positive / affirmative focus
- Commitment to being open and vulnerable
- Commitment to transformation
- Willingness / flexibility / adaptability
- Projection of positive energy and imagining a positive outcome—as if planting seeds—in your future.

Creating "GOD Project" Intentions Support

In many of the transformational programs, courses, and workshops I have taken since the 1980s, the following success mindset left an impression on me. Though various people and organizations state it in different ways, here is the central idea:

If this _____ (book, program, project) were to be _____ (immensely, wildly, greatly) successful, what would you experience?

Now, it is your turn. Answer the following:

If this _____ (book, program, project) were to be _____ (immensely, wildly, greatly) successful, I would experience _____.

Before going within, with your thinking mind make notes of the type of things you think you want to experience—and state them in an affirmative way. An example of an *affirmative way* means instead of stating *"not* being as confused" (what you *don't* want and using the word *not)*—state *clarity* (what you *do* want). Another example: Instead of stating *"not* being so disconnected from God"—state *experiencing connection with God.* List anything that comes to mind. Journal your responses in the space provided below.

My thinking mind response: What I want to experience is ...

Journal (continued)

While you most likely answered the query easily and "off the top of your head" (from your thinking mind), the intention now is to go within and seek a deeper answer (one that comes from your Heart Soul).

Using **GETTING GOD™ ~ "The GOD Project"** book and **The Guidebook** as an example of a subject for my intentions, after going within, my responses were:

> If **GETTING GOD™ ~ "The GOD Project"** book and **The Guidebook** were to be *amazingly* and *wildly* successful, I would experience:
>
> - Inner joy
> - Being of service
> - Deep sense of humility
> - Joy and gratitude in knowing that I assisted others in an improved perception of one of the most foundational, pivotal, important, and core relationships—their relationship with God and, ultimately, with themselves and others
> - An enhanced perception of an ever-improving expansion and deepening of my perception of my own relationship with God, myself, and others
> - An expansion of my personal, intimate experience of the True Nature of God

NOTE: After going within, here is what came forward as my one of intentions:

> My intention is to share what I have learned, developed, and provided within **GETTING GOD™ ~ "The GOD Project"** book and **The Guidebook** to assist in the raising of my level of consciousness / vibrations in service to raising the consciousness / vibration of others, our nation, and ultimately, our planet.

Going Within to Discover Your "GOD Project" Intention(s)

Regardless of what your mind / mind influencing your body / mind as your body is telling you, it is important to set an intention within and simply trust the process.

Steps

- Preparation: Outer & Inner Environments
- Set your session intention.

  Example: "My intention is to go within and discover my intention(s) for my 'GOD Project.'"
- Journal your responses below.

My "GOD Project" Intention(s):

Journal (continued)

Optional: Journal Queries

After journaling about your intentions, you can also journal as much as you would like regarding your experience of your intention-setting session, impressions, discoveries, lessons learned, insights, epiphanies, surprises, musings …

Some questions to consider answering or writing about:

- *Did you note similar responses from your initial thinking mind and after going within? Different responses?*

- *Did any of the responses surprise you?*

- You can journal your responses below.

Journal

Journal

Affirmations

Intentions can be a springboard for affirmations. Affirmations are positive and supportive declarative statements. The purpose of using affirmations is to anchor or ground the positive energy of your intentions in the present and catapult them into the future. Additionally, by using some specific wording, your affirmations can support greater energetic alignment with your intentions.

There is a huge energetic difference between wishful thinking and affirmations. Wishful thinking begins with words such as *I want to, I hope to, It would be nice if*, and so on. The energy with these types of statements is wistful, weak, and tentative, and leaves room for ambiguity and doubt. Those types of words imply a longing and pining for something to happen. Those words also leave a lot of space for the energy of something *not* to happen because the implied energy is "It would be nice if _____ happens, *but ...*"

Every time the word or energy of *but* is used in intentions, affirmations, and visioning, you create conflicting and/or competing energy. Conflicting and competing energy negates affirmations. You do not want to leave any invitation for conflicting energy when creating affirmations—or any other kind of positive imagery work.

To create energetically strong affirmations, some specific wording can be beneficial. I found the following helpful when creating my affirmations:

- Begin each sentence with "I Am." This is done to call forward the God / Spirit / Highest Power Within and align it with the God / Spirit / Highest Power Throughout. It also supports being in the here and now.

- State the action word or verb in the present / present-progressive tense (using verbs that end with –*ing,* such as enjoying, playing, dancing). This supports anchoring the energy in the here and now and paves the way, energetically, for your future.

Another key element of affirmations is to keep them somewhat within the realm of possibility for you—at least halfway or, as some workshops, conferences and training programs suggest—50 percent or more believable to you. For example, "I Am graduating from medical school with honors" would not be an appropriate or fitting affirmation for me because I have no aptitude to become a medical doctor and am squeamish at the sight of blood. That affirmation is *not* within the realm of possibility nor is it even remotely believable for me.

Having said that, I do believe in miracles. I always avail myself to being open and receptive for miracles within my life at all times. I feel it is important for you to do the same.

Energetic Qualities of Affirmations

- Being positive / supportive / uplifting / affirming
- Commitment to transforming
- Openness / willingness / flexibility / adaptability
- Creation with "as if" energy—envisioning and stating something as though it is already happening here and now to "ground" it as if planting seeds
- Grounds positive energy in the present
- Projection of positive energy and imagining a positive outcome in your future
- Propels positive energy into the future

Examples of Affirmations

- "I Am open and receptive to transforming my relationship with God in an easy and gentle manner."
- "I Am open to discovering the True Nature of God."

- "I Am enjoying sharing my love with God and the experience of knowing God's Love for me."

- "I Am enjoying a joy-filled, loving, supportive relationship with God—and am assisting others in enjoying the same."

- "I Am loving God as God loves me—fully, deeply, unconditionally."

- "I Am experiencing the beauty and the power of my loving relationship with God—and am assisting others in experiencing God's loving too."

NOTE: What you write below can also be used when creating your ideal scenario (see previous chapter) because ideal scenarios are filled with your affirmations. As mentioned in the previous chapter, creating ideal scenarios is optional and it is a visually creative way of approaching, creating and energizing affirmations. However, taking time to follow the points explained in this segment on affirmations, I believe, is vital and foundationally imperative for the success of your project. Laying this groundwork was important for me and for the success of my "GOD Project."

Now it is time for you to create your "GOD Project" affirmations.

I Am

I Am

I Am

I Am

Vision Creation

I define a *vision creation* as affirmations that are compiled in a way that creates a positive energetic response within. I view it as a trade-in and upgrade from one's old victim story. Your vision creation can be a list of affirmations or a narrative. You can add color, pictures, or anything you can think of that will enhance the positive energy you are consciously creating. (See **Example of a Vision Creation** below.)

Again, I do believe in miracles, and I want to be open and receptive to them at all times. That is why I like to include a supportive *addendum* at the end of my intentions, affirmations, ideal scenarios, and vision stories.

Some training programs I have attended use various addendum statements—or none at all. Below is a template you can use to create your own.

I _____ (embrace / claim / affirm) this, or something even more _____ (grand / magnificent / delightful), for the _____ (greatest / maximum / highest / grandest) _____ (benefit / blessing / outcome) for myself and all others.

Energetic Qualities of Vision Stories

- Being positive / supportive / uplifting / affirming / enthusiastic
- Commitment to transforming
- Openness / willingness / flexibility / adaptability

- Creation with "as if" energy—envisioning and stating something as though it is already happening here and now to "ground" it as if planting seeds
- Grounds positive energy in the present
- Projection of positive energy and imagining a positive outcome in your future
- Propels positive energy into the future
- Multisensory imagery

Example of a Vision Creation

I'm excited! I Am experiencing an amazingly loving relationship with God. I Am experiencing God's Love for me. The experience of a close and loving connection with God is powerful and real. I Am more aware of God's presence in my life and in the life of others. I Am guided and sustained by God's Love. I Am being supported and guided. God adores me. I Am feeling secure knowing and experiencing God's Love as real. God and I are one.

Each and every day, my awareness of God's Love for me grows stronger and stronger. As I am reading spiritually oriented books, meditating, and praying, the True Nature of God and God's Love becomes more clear and real for me. As I Am interacting with people, I Am enjoying looking for God's Divine Essence within them. As I Am practicing seeing and experiencing God's loving presence within them, I Am experiencing connection—The Oneness. God is real for me.

I affirm all of this and even more—much greater, more

delightful, and more amazing than what I could ever possibly imagine—for the maximum benefit for myself, others, and the entire planet.

Now it is time for you to create your vision. Journal using the space below.

Journal

Journal

Journal

I _____ (embrace / claim / affirm) this, or something even more _____ (grand / magnificent / delightful), for the _____ (greatest / maximum / highest / grandest) _____ (benefit / blessing / outcome) for myself and all others.

Chapter 6

Divining

I consider the tool of divining to be my personal and portable "lie detector." Like a *lie detector*, it discerns truth / resonance and falsehood / dissonance. Additionally, divining is a tool that can be used to discover and discern energetic blocks and imbalances that are present within your subconscious / unconscious and your energy field.

In the context of the "GOD Project," divining is used to discover what negative and/or challenging beliefs / programs, blocks and imbalances are present that contribute to a perceived "distance" between you and God. Additionally, you can use divining techniques to discover which positive beliefs / programs are missing—and contributing to your perception of not experiencing your desired positive relationship with God.

It is important to understand that divining your way into your subconscious / unconscious is intended to be a process that is gentle, supportive, and guided by God / Spirit / Highest Power. It is a way to connect the aspect of God Within to that of God Throughout. There are "check-ins" after each and every step along the way—to make sure you can proceed without any major disruptive upheaval—on any and all levels. It is important to follow the detailed protocols to make sure this is not, in any way, a disruptive process.

Groundwork: Establish a Baseline

Establishing a baseline is an essential process for each and every divining session. With divining, a baseline of resonance (truth) and dissonance (falsehood) can be discerned. They are also the first things that must be discerned.

Upon questioning, if there is resonance (truth) present, no marked movements of micro muscles are detected; electrical energy flows freely and the muscles will test "strong." This indicates that there is no disruption or obstruction of the flow of energy and no blocked energy. It is equivalent to getting an affirmative response.

Upon questioning, if there is dissonance (falsehood) present, marked micro muscle movements are detected. This indicates a disruption or obstruction in the flow of electrical energy, resulting in blocked energy, causing the muscles to test "weak." It is equivalent to getting a "not-affirmative" response.

After a clear baseline has been established, you can begin testing anything (food, supplement, statement, idea) to see if it is **energetically** congruent / beneficial / present for you and your energy system and presents a *strong* or *yes* response. Additionally, you can decipher whether something is *energetically* incongruent / not beneficial / not present for you and your energy system, resulting in a *weak* or *no* response.

If you are not able to discern your *yes* and *no* response, see **What to Do If You Are Not Able to Discern Your Yes and No** on pages 67-68.

Divining Techniques and How to Establish Baselines

There are numerous techniques for divining. In this chapter I will share some methods that require two people and other methods that you can do by yourself.

While there are more techniques within each method, what I am sharing will provide you with a variety of ways to easily explore, practice, and master divining—either with a partner or by yourself. Detailed steps for each method presented are included. Also included is information regarding what establishing your baselines will look like and what you can expect to experience for each of the divining techniques.

At any time during the entire process,

1. Stop if you meet resistance,

2. Continue when ready, and again,

3. *Always* stop if you meet any resistance at any stage.

Two-Person Divining and Establishing Baselines

The first three techniques are for divining while working with a partner.

Outstretched Arm Divining (Standing or Sitting)

Tester: Begin by having the test taker (testee) outstretch either arm to the side of his or her body.

- Set your intention to clearly and easily establish the testee's *strong* (or *yes*) and *weak* (or *no*) baselines. (See below.)

- If testee is standing, stand in front of the testee's raised arm; if testee is seated, sit in chair in front of the testee's raised arm.

  - You can also stand behind the testee.

  - Whichever you choose, continue testing consistently, using the same procedures throughout.

- Place one hand on the shoulder of the side of the testee's outstretched arm; the other hand should be on the testee's outstretched forearm.

- While divining, do not exert brute force. Lightly apply pressure on the testee's forearm. (This is not a test of anyone's physical force, will power, and/or resistance strength.)

Testee:

- Set your intention to clearly and easily establish your *strong* (or *yes)* and *weak* (or *no)* baselines.

- Do not exert tense resistance. Use mild resistance. (Again, this is not a test of anyone's will power, physical strength, and / or resistance strength.)

Establish Your Baselines[2]: *Strong* or *Yes*

Goal / Intention: To get a clear response without muscle strain, force, and so on. While divining, the testee's arm position should remain *strong* after stating something that is *true*.

- Testee: With an outstretched arm, say something that is *true* while maintaining mild resistance. For example:

- My name is _____.

- Tester: Lightly apply pressure on the testee's outstretched forearm.

- Testee: Continue to maintain mild resistance.

Baseline Response: *Strong* or *Yes*. If—while stating something that is true and divining—the testee's arm position remains *strong* and does not release, this would indicate a *yes* = *truthful / congruent* statement.

The tester and testee can now discern what the testee's *yes / affirmative / congruent* divining response baseline response looks like and feels like.

NOTE: If testee's arm position becomes *weak* (or *no)* when testing a *true* statement or *strong* (or *yes)* when testing a *false*

---

[2]For the remainder of ***The Guidebook***, refer to ***Establish Your Baselines (All Divining Sessions)*** (p. 67) for the steps regarding establishing a clear *strong* or *yes* response and a clear *weak* or *no* response when divining. See individual methods for how each *strong* or *yes* and *weak* or *no* will look and feel.

statement, or if you get what you perceive as a lack of any discernable response—stop! Refer to **What to Do If You Are Not Able to Discern Your Yes and No** on pages 67-68.[3]

After every step:

Divining Continuation Protocol[4] (Two-Person or One-Person Methods)

- Divine if you can proceed.

- If testee's arm / forearm position / finger link / finger position remains *strong* (*yes*), continue.

- If testee's arm / forearm position / finger link / finger position becomes *weak* (*no*), refer to **What to Do If You Get a No (Weak) to Proceed** on pages 68-69.

Establish Your Baselines[5]: *Weak or No*

Goal / Intention: To get a clear *weak* or *no* without muscle strain, force, and so on. While divining, the testee's arm hold should become *weak* and essentially collapse its position after stating something *false*.

- Testee: With an outstretched arm, say something that is *not true* while maintaining mild resistance. For example:

  My name is _____. (State a false name.)

- Tester: Lightly apply pressure on the testee's outstretched forearm.

- Testee: Continue to maintain mild resistance.

---

[3] Always refer to **What to Do If You Are Not Able to Discern Your Yes and No** on pp. 67-68 if you cannot discern responses.
[4] After every step, follow this **Divining Continuation Protocol**.
[5] Reminder: For the remainder of **The Guidebook**, refer to **Establish Your Baselines (All Divining Sessions)** (p. 67) for the steps regarding establishing a clear *strong* or *yes* response and clear *weak* or *no* response when divining. See individual methods for how each *strong* or *yes* and *weak* or *no* will look and feel.

Baseline Response: *Weak* **or** *No.* If—while stating something that is not true and divining—the testee's arm position becomes *weak* and does not remain strong, this would indicate a *no* = *not truthful / incongruent* statement.

The tester and testee have now established what the testee's *no / not affirmative / incongruent* divining baseline looks like and feels like. Additionally, via divining, the tester and testee can now discern between *yes / truthful / congruent* and *no / not truthful / incongruent* responses.

Forearm (Standing or Sitting) Divining

Tester: Begin by having the test taker (testee) either stand up or sit down.

- If testee is standing or sitting in a chair with no armrest, have testee raise the forearm of their choosing along the front side of their body, to a point halfway between their hip and shoulder.

- If testee is sitting in a chair with an armrest, have testee rest their elbow joint bone on armrest, with the forearm at a 45-degree angle to the armrest.

NOTE: The tester can actually apply light pressure on the forearm in the direction toward the testee's shoulder or on the forearm toward the hip / armrest. Once you use one direction of pressure, keep the direction consistent for the remainder of the session.

Tester and Testee

- Set your intentions to clearly and easily establish the testee's *strong* or *yes* and *weak* or *no* baselines.

- Tester—Do not exert brute force; Testee—Do not exert tense resistance.

Establish Your Baselines —
Forearm (Standing or Sitting) Divining

Baseline Response: *Strong* or *Yes*. Regardless of the direction of pressure, if—while stating something that is true and divining—the testee's arm position remains *strong* and does not release, this would indicate a *yes = truthful / congruent* statement.

The tester and testee have now established what the testee's *yes / affirmative / congruent* divining baseline looks like and feels like.

Baseline Response: *Weak* or *No*. Regardless of the direction of pressure, if—while stating something that is not true and divining—the testee's arm position becomes *weak* and does not remain strong, this would indicate a *no = not truthful / incongruent* statement.

The tester and testee have now established what the testee's *no / not affirmative / incongruent* divining baseline looks like and feels like. Additionally, via divining, the tester and testee can now discern between *yes / truthful / congruent* and *no / not truthful / incongruent* responses.

Lying Down (with Outstretched Arm or Forearm)

Tester: Begin by having the test taker (testee) lie down on a flat surface. Leaving the back of the arm and elbow joint bone on the flat surface, have the testee raise a forearm and hand straight up or just raise the forearm up toward the ceiling.

NOTE: As with the *Forearm (Standing or Sitting)* technique above, the tester can actually apply light pressure on the forearm in the direction toward the testee's shoulder or on the forearm toward the hip / flat surface. As always, once you use one direction of pressure, keep the direction consistent for the remainder of the session.

Establish Your Baselines —
Lying Down (with Outstretched Arm/Forearm)

Baseline Response: *Strong* or *Yes*. Regardless of the direction of pressure, if—while stating something that is true and divining— the testee's arm position remains *strong* and does not release, this would indicate a *yes = truthful / congruent* statement.

The tester and testee can now discern what the testee's *yes / affirmative / congruent* divining baseline response looks like and feels like.

Baseline Response: *Weak* or *No*. Regardless of the direction of pressure, if—while stating something that is not true and divining—the testee's arm position becomes *weak* and does not remain strong, this would indicate a *no = not truthful / incongruent* statement.

The tester and testee have now established what the testee's *no / not affirmative / incongruent* divining baseline looks like and feels like. Additionally, via divining, the tester and testee can now discern between *yes / truthful / congruent* and *no / not truthful / incongruent* responses.

Divining by Yourself and Establishing Baselines

Divining without a partner is another option. You can divine by yourself using one of the following techniques.

Interlocking Fingers

Begin by interlocking your pinkie fingers together. Actually, you can do this with any of your fingers—except for the thumbs. Additionally, you can form interlocking rings with your fingers by interlocking either middle finger and thumbs or index fingers and thumbs.

Establish Your Baselines — Interlocking Fingers

Baseline Responses: *Strong* or *Yes*. Regardless of which fingers you use, if—while stating something truthful and divining—your interlocking fingers' hold / link remains *strong* and does not release (or "break") with mild resistance and gentle pressure, this would indicate a *yes = truthful / congruent* statement.

You can now discern what your *yes / affirmative / congruent* divining response baseline response looks like and feels like.

Baseline Response: *Weak* or *No*. If—while stating something *not truthful*—your interlocking fingers' hold / link becomes *weak* and "breaks" with mild resistance and gentle pressure, this would indicate a *no = not truthful / incongruent* statement.

You have now established what your *no / not affirmative / incongruent* divining baseline looks like and feels like. Additionally, via divining, you can now discern between *yes / truthful / congruent* and *no / not truthful / incongruent* responses.

Index Indicator

Using either hand's index finger, place the same hand's middle finger on top of your index finger. Apply gentle pressure from the middle finger on the top of the index finger, while using mild resistance.

Establish Your Baselines — Index Indicator

Baseline Responses: *Strong* or *Yes*. Regardless of which hand's fingers you use, if—while stating something that is true and divining—your index finger remains *strong* and does not bend, this would indicate a *yes* = *truthful / congruent* statement.

You can now discern what your *yes / affirmative / congruent* divining response baseline response looks like and feels like.

Baseline Response: *Weak* or *No*. If—while stating something not truthful and divining—your index finger becomes weak and bends, this would indicate a *no* = not truthful / incongruent statement.

You have now established what your *no / not affirmative / incongruent* divining baseline looks like and feels like. Additionally, via divining, you can now discern between *yes / truthful / congruent* and *no / not truthful / incongruent* responses.

Armrest Press

Using either arm, place your elbow joint bone on the armrest of a chair with your forearm extending across your chest pointing to the other armrest. Apply gentle pressure between the wrist and elbow of the extended forearm. (An alternative: Place your elbow joint bone on the armrest of a chair with your forearm pointing toward the ceiling.)

Establish Your Baselines — Armrest Press

Baseline Response: *Strong* or *Yes*. If—while stating something that is true and divining—the forearm's position remains *strong* and does not bend toward your lap and / or the armrest), this would indicate a *yes* = *truthful / congruent* statement.

You can now discern what your *yes / affirmative / congruent* divining response baseline response looks like and feels like.

Baseline Response: *Weak* or *No*. If—while stating something *not truthful* and divining—the forearm's position becomes *weak* and bends toward your lap (or the armrest), this would indicate a *no = false / incongruent* statement.

You have now established what your *no / not affirmative / incongruent* divining baseline looks like and feels like. Additionally, via divining, you can now discern between *yes / truthful / congruent* and *no / not truthful / incongruent* responses.

Rocking

You can start by either standing or sitting still. For beginners, I recommend starting with standing. (Some people believe you should find "north" and intend for "true" statements to give a "northern" indication. I, however, believe one gets what they believe, and I do not believe that step is necessary. It never became a necessary factor for me.)

Establish Your Baselines — Rocking

Baseline Responses: *Strong* or *Yes*. If—while stating something that is true and divining—your body (or torso, if sitting) sways *forward*, this would indicate a *yes = truthful / congruent* statement.

You can now discern what your *yes / affirmative / congruent* divining response baseline response looks like and feels like.

Baseline Response: *Weak* or *No*. If—while stating something *not truthful* and divining—your body (or torso, if sitting) sways *backward*, this would indicate a *no = false / incongruent* statement.

You have now established what your *no / not affirmative / incongruent* divining baseline looks like and feels like. Additionally, via divining, you can now discern between *yes / truthful / congruent* and *no / not truthful / incongruent* responses.

Pendulum

Another way of discerning a *yes / congruent* from a *no / incongruent* via divining is by using a pendulum.

A pendulum can be any weighted object at the end of a string or chain. It can be used as a divining tool to detect micro muscle movements and vibrations, which affects the directional swinging of a pendulum.

Sometimes mastering this technique can take a while. Mastery requires your commitment and/or intention to acquire proficiency, time, focus, and practice.

Important: It is not the pendulum "saying" *yes* or *no*—and it is never meant to be approached in a "go ask the pendulum" manner. A pendulum is simply a means or an instrument, like the lie detector, that can assist you in reading your own energy field via divining.

Do not confuse the pendulum or the use of a pendulum—while divining in a transformational context—with an Ouija Board. Ouija Boards, and the energy "invoked" and transmitted while using one, and divining with a pendulum as a tool to discern what is energetically congruent or incongruent, are *not* the same thing. In my opinion, the Ouija Board is a gateway for negative / darker energies—and I do not want to invite that kind of energy into my life and energy field.

How to Divine Using a Pendulum

For Beginners …

Important: If you get an indication to use the pendulum during your "GOD Project," it is imperative that you first master getting and discerning your clear *yes / congruent* and clear *no / incongruent* responses.

> **Goal / Intention**: To get a clear indication of what your *yes / congruent* and *no / incongruent* responses looks like and feels like while divining with a pendulum.
>
> - With the pendulum in front of you, hold the top of the chain (away from the weighted object) between your index finger and thumb or between your index and middle fingers. Make sure there is room for the weighted object to swing.
>
> **NOTE**: The vibration of *yes / congru*ent will move the pendulum one direction while the vibration of *no / incongruent* will move the pendulum in an opposite direction.
>
> **Examples**:
>
> - A *yes / congruent* response could be an up / down (north / south) movement—the same as a head nodding *yes*.
>
> - A *no / incongruent* response could be a left / right (east / west) movement—the same as a head movement of *no*.
>
> Or …
>
> - A *yes / congruent* response could be a clockwise movement of the pendulum.
>
> - A *no / incongruent* response could be a counter clockwise movement of the pendulum.
>
> Remember: Be open to whatever movement comes forward for you.

Pendulum Divining Practice Techniques

- Set your intention to clearly and easily establish what your *yes / true / congruent* pendulum direction looks like and feels like.

    o Think or say out loud: "Yes! Yes! Yes!"

    o See which way the pendulum moves (up or down; left or right; circle to the left; circle to the right; and so on). The direction of this movement indicates a *yes = true / congruent* response.

- Set your intention to clearly and easily establish what your *no / false / incongruent* pendulum direction looks like and feels like.

    o Think or say out loud: "No! No! No! No!"

    o The pendulum should move in the opposite direction of your established *yes* response. The direction of this movement indicates a *no = false / incongruent* response.

NOTE: While you may notice little to no movement, be patient with yourself and your process—and keep practicing.

Pendulum Divining

With the pendulum in front of you, hold the top of the chain (away from the weighted object) between your index and thumb or index and middle finger. Make sure there is room for the weighted object to swing.

Establish Your Baselines — Pendulum Divining

Baseline Response: *Strong* or *Yes*. If—while stating something that is true and divining—the pendulum moves in your established *yes* directional movement, this would indicate a *yes = truthful / congruent* statement.

You can now discern what your *yes / true / congruent* divining response baseline response looks like and feels like.

Baseline Response: *Weak* **or** *No*. If—while stating something *not truthful* and divining—the pendulum moves in your established *no* directional movement, this would indicate a *no = false / incongruent* statement.

You have now established what your *no / false / incongruent* divining baseline looks like and feels like. Additionally, via divining, you can now discern between *yes / truthful / congruent* and *no / not truthful / incongruent* responses.

NOTE: Though not a requirement, meditation is an essential tool to have and to incorporate into one's *Spiritual Tool Kit*. I have found that meditating either before or after any type of divining session has been extremely beneficial for me.

My Pendulum Experience

Initially, I had a challenging time getting a clear *yes* and *no* with a pendulum. I have noticed the same challenge with some of my friends and clients. Upon exploration, I divined, using other techniques, that I (and those who were similarly challenged) had subconscious programs regarding this type of "divining" as "evil," "ungodly," and so on. After clearing these subconscious programs and with much practice establishing a baseline with the pendulum, I am happy to report that I (and others I support) now can easily discern *yes* and *no* by using a pendulum. The pendulum is now one of the major "go-to" techniques I use with myself and with others.

Summary of Divining Steps with Protocols

Below you will find all of the recommended steps and protocols that will assist you with the divining process during your "GOD Project."

Beginning Session Protocol for All Divining Sessions

For this to be a process of ease and gentleness, it is imperative to establish and adhere to a certain protocol for each and every divining session.

- Preparation: Outer & Inner Environments
- Invoke God / Spirit / Highest Power and say a heartfelt prayer.
- State your clearing and release intention (verbally or silently).
- Discern which divining method to use by using your intuition and / or your level of comfort.
- Establish your baselines.

Establish Your Baselines — All Divining Sessions

- State your intention to discern, with ease and clarity, your divining baselines.

- Establish your *strong / yes / congruent* baseline.

  - State something that is *true / factual*. Divine.

  - If you test *strong* or *yes*,

- You have established what your *yes / true / congruent* statement looks like and feels like while divining.

  - If you get test *weak* or *no* when testing the *true / factual* statement—stop!

    - Refer to **What to Do If You Are Not Able to Discern Your Yes and No** on page see below.

- Establish your *weak / no / incongruent* baseline.

  - State something that is *not true*. Divine.

  - If you test *weak* or *no* regarding this *not truthful* statement,

    - You have established your *no / false / incongruent* baseline and

    - You can now discern how your *yes* and *no* feels like and looks like when divining.

  - If you are not able to discern between your *yes* and *no*—stop!

    - Refer to **What to Do If You Are Not Able to Discern Your Yes and No** (below).

What to Do If You Are Not Able to Discern Your Yes and No

- Drink water. Wait a few minutes and try again.

- Set your intention to experience clarity with discerning *yes* and *no* while divining, in service to your growth, healing, and upliftment.

- This time, think or say out loud: "Yes! Yes! Yes! Yes!" Test for a *yes* baseline. Confirm by stating a true statement. You should experience the same baseline results.

- Now think or say out loud: "No! No! No! No!" Test for a *no* baseline. Confirm by stating a false statement. You should experience the same baseline results.

- Practice, and be patient with yourself.

Divining Continuation Protocol

- Divine if you can proceed.

  - If you test *strong* or *yes*, continue.

  - Ask if you are able to clear and release something at this time. Divine.

    - If you get a *yes* (*strong*), proceed.

    - If you get a *no* (*weak*)—stop![6]

    - Refer to **What to Do If You Get a No (Weak) to Proceed** (see below).

What to Do If You Get a No (Weak) to Proceed

- Drink a glass of water.

- After waiting a few minutes, try again.

  - If you still get a *no* (*weak*), try again another day.

  - Do not continue until you get a *yes* (*strong*) response.

- Additionally, consider

  - going within,

  - praying for clarity and for assistance from God / Spirit / Highest Power,

  - restating your healing intention,

---

[6] From now on, if after getting repeated *no* (weak) responses to your correct name when attempting to establish your baseline, whether to proceed, or that a clearing took place—stop. Refer to **What to Do If You Get a No (Weak) to Proceed.**

- being patient and gentle with yourself, and

- persisting ... another day.

Divining Which Statement to Clear First ... Next ... Next ...

Using divining testing, discern which statement to energetically address, clear, and release first, next, and so on.

Divining Statements Protocol

- Follow the **Beginning Session Protocol for All Divining Sessions** (see page 66).

- Referring to the statement charts in Chapter 10, ask God / Spirit / Highest Power which statement to clear first and discern via divining:

    - "Lack of Positive Statements": Y/N?

    - "Negative / Challenged Statements": Y/N?

- Within the category indicated, ask God / Spirit / Highest Power which of the follow to clear first and discern via divining:

    - Group: A (Y/N?), B (Y/N?), C (Y/N?)

    - Number: 1? (Y/N?), 2? (Y/N?), 3? (Y/N?), 4? (Y/N?), 5? (Y/N?)

- Check the "Challenged" box corresponding to the statement indicated.

- Divine to see if more information is needed (see **Divining for More Information** and **Divining for More Information Protocol** below).

    - Reminder: If you are prompted to divine for more information and if there is an indication that the energetic statement was inherited, you can choose to do one of the following within the statement's Challenged box:

        - Circle the check.

        - Place an asterisk or the initial "I" next to the check.

- Create a way to designate the statement as inherited within the *Challenged* box.

• If, after divining, you are given a go-ahead to proceed, begin Step 5 (see page 179).

NOTE: Within one divining statements session, you may move back and forth between both "Negative / Challenged" and "Lack of Positive" statements. (Additionally, when the time comes to do the clearing and release process, there may be times when you will be able to clear and release multiple energetic statements; other times you'll only clear and release one or two.)

Be patient with yourself and your process.

Divining for More Information

There were times during my own "GOD Project" that I intuitively sensed I needed to know more about the origin of or experience that caused the block or imbalance. At those times, I would ask God / Spirit / Highest Power something akin to this: Is there any detail / specific / additional information I need to know about this? If I received a *strong* or *yes* indication during divining, I would ask Spirit to reveal to me what I needed to know.

Too Much Information or Need to Know?

There were other times that, although I may have been curious about the details surrounding a block and/or imbalance, no additional information was indicated or required for me (and subsequently for my clients) to know in order for the clearing and releasing to take place.

I believe this is the reason: Some people may be quite "head-y." (At times, I tend to be very immersed within my own "head.") Some may still want to be attached to their "victim story." Their thinking / ego mind "wants a bone to chew on"; this "munching mind" wants something to gnaw on. Many times, when I ask God / Spirit / Highest Power if I (or my clients) need to know any additional or detailed information, I receive a *no* when divining.

I view receiving a *no* as a directive from God / Spirit / Highest Power and believe there are several reasons for this. It supports an easy and gentle rebalancing by:

- Creating separation from one's "victim" story if one is "head-y"

- Not feeding a "munching mind"

- Attempting to prevent picking at and revisiting any former wound(s)—which only serves to uphold and/or perhaps reactivate the wound(s)' vibration.

- Allowing for whatever was cleared and released to remain cleared and released.

Divining for More Information Protocol

- Ask: *Do I need to know more information about this (in the context of the statement you are focusing on) at this time?* Divine.

- If you receive a *no* response about needing to know additional information, proceed to the protocols for the clearing modality indicated.

- If you receive a *yes* response,

    ○ Ask something like *"What information do I need to know at this time?"*

    ○ Use your intuition to be open to information to appear to you in the form of signs, symbols, words, colors, sounds, the experience of emotions, and so on.

- Ask if the issue was inherited.

    ○ If you get a *yes*, ask: *"What information do I need to know at this time?"* For example: maternal or paternal side? Male or female?

    ○ Use your intuition to be open to information to appear to you in the form of signs, symbols, words, colors, sounds, the experience of emotions, and so on.

    ○ Make a notation on the chart's *Challenged* box of an inherited energetic.

PART II

My "GOD Project"

Chapter 7

Step 1: Evaluate and Determine

Before beginning any transformational program, I believe it is a good practice to evaluate where you are now and where you want to be. The information gleaned from this process will provide you information of your before, during, and after "GOD Project" progress. This information will be helpful to refer back to witness how much progress and transformation has actually taken place at any given time along the way.

If you have already written your responses in Chapter 5, you can:

- Leave your answers in Chapter 5 and complete the portions of this step that you have not yet done,

- Copy your previous responses and insert them here to keep your project contained to one area for easy reference, or

- Update and refine your initial responses by doing them again and noting them in this section.

Evaluate

Start by using the following as the baseline question and journal your responses using the space provided:

When you think about God and how you perceive your relationship with God, how do you feel?

Journal

How do you perceive your relationship with God now?

Describe your perceived stress or level of challenge now.

Stress / Challenge Evaluation

Find a quiet time and space. Take a moment to consciously and energetically connect with your body through deep breathing. Connect with your feelings. Silently read the questions below. Journal your responses.

On a scale of 1–10 (1 = ever so slightly stressed / challenged; 10 = deeply, disturbingly stressed / challenged), rate the following:

_____ *How much of a challenge is / how much stress are you currently experiencing with your perceived relationship with God?*

_____ *When you think about the current status of your relationship with God, what amount of stress do you experience within?*

_____ *How blocked / closed off do you feel regarding your relationship with God?*

_____ *How blocked / closed off do you feel regarding receiving love from God?*

_____ *How blocked / closed off do you feel regarding sending love to God?*

_____ *How much frustration do you feel regarding your relationship with God?*

_____ *How much shame do you feel regarding your perceived current state of your relationship with God?*

_____ *How hopeless do you feel regarding the "improvement" of this relationship?*

Add other questions, comments and / or observations about your stresses and challenges.

Journal

Journal

Journal

Determine What You Want to Experience

With any project or experiment, it is always a good idea to establish what direction you want to be going in—what you are working toward. A powerful tool to use to help set your energetic direction is to consciously establish what your intentions (energetically infused goals) are for your "GOD Project." For example, you can establish intentions for the experience of the project, desired end results, the improved quality of the relationship you are seeking, and so on.

Going Within to Discover Your "GOD Project" Intentions

- Preparation: Outer & Inner Environments
- Set your session intention. Key at this time is setting an intention to connect within, and simply trusting the process, regardless of what your mind / mind influencing your body (your mind as your body) is telling you.

  Example: My intention is to go within and discover the answer to the following question: *If my "GOD Project" were to be _____ (immensely, wildly, greatly) successful, I would I like to experience ...*

- Journal your responses.

Journal

Journal

Based on what you wrote, create clear and concise intention statements for your key project. Journal your responses.

My intention is to …

My intention is to …

My intention is to …

My intention is to …

My intention is to …

- Upon emerging from this session, journal as much as you would like about your experience of your session, discoveries, lessons learned, takeaways, insights, epiphanies, surprises, musings ...

- Additionally, here are some questions to consider answering or journaling about:

  - Did any of your responses surprise you?

  - Upon reflection, if another intention comes forward for you, write it down.

  - If, after reading your intentions, they do not have any "juicy," power-filled energy for you, consider rewriting them until they do.

Journal

Journal

Journal

Affirmations

Using your intentions, create your "GOD Project" affirmations.

- Preparation: Outer & Inner Environments
- Set your session intention. Example: My intention is to go within and create "GOD Project" affirmations.
- Journal your responses.

I Am ...

I Am ...

I Am ...

I Am ...

Creating Your Vision

Using your affirmations above, create your vision for your "GOD Project."

- Preparation: Outer & Inner Environments
- Set your session intention. Example: My intention is to go within and create my vision for my "GOD Project" and for my relationship with God.
- Journal your responses.

Journal

Journal

Journal

I _____ (embrace / claim / affirm) this, or something even more _____ (grand / magnificent / delightful), for the _____ (greatest / maximum / highest / grandest) _____ (benefit / blessing / outcome) for myself and all others.[7]

---

[7]This statement can also be used after your intentions, affirmations, and ideal scenarios.

Chapter 8

STEP 2: EXPLORE

I believe it is imperative to consciously explore your memory to trace the root cause of your sense and perception of "separation" from God / Spirit / Highest Power: what you learned about God, how you learned it, and from whom. In this section, you will examine your indoctrinations, perceptions, characteristics of your most challenging parental figure, and discover which of the same challenging characteristics you may have projected onto your perception of God.

Indoctrinations

Whether you realized it or not, you were indoctrinated by a variety of sources as you were growing up. First, you'll look at your religious influences and then your religious influences from your family of origin. After considering each statement, journal your responses.

Religion / Church Indoctrination

How was God described in books, songs, and movies you were exposed to while growing up?

Journal

How were you, in relation to God, described?

Family of Origin Indoctrination

If your mother was present during your upbringing, how did she describe God? (If your mother was not present, how did the most influential female figure in your life while growing up describe God?)

If your father was present during your upbringing, how did he describe God? (If your father was not present, how did the most influential male figure in your life describe God while you were growing up?)

Perceptions of Relationships with God

The ways in which your parental influences related to God as well as your perceptions of their relationships with God affected your perception of your own relationship with God. In this next section, you will consider those influences and journal your thoughts about them.

Perceptions of Parental Figures' Relationships with God

If you were to describe the relationship your mother (or the most influential female in your life while growing up) had with God—based purely on your perspective and perceptions—how would you describe it?

If you were to describe the relationship your father (or the most influential male in your life while growing up) had with God—based purely on your perspective and perceptions—how would you describe it?

Perceptions of Your Relationship with God

If you were to describe your relationship with God while you were growing up—based purely on your perspective and perceptions—how would you describe it?

Today, if you were to describe your relationship with God—based purely on your perspective and perceptions—how would you describe it?

Looking back, in what ways did your relationship with God reflect and resemble your relationship with your most challenging parental figure?

Challenging Characteristics and Relationships

Challenging relationship characteristics can be repeated and experienced in multiple relationships. Explore the challenging common denominator(s) within your relationships—in general. Journal your responses.

Journal

Challenging Parental Figure

Which relationship did you find to be more challenging while you were growing up: the relationship with your mother (or an influential female figure) or with your father (or an influential male figure)? Answer here.

How would you describe the characteristics of the person you were more challenged by? Journal your response.

Journal

Challenging God Figure

Does your most challenging parental figure or influential person possess the same characteristics that you attribute to God? Answer here.

According to your experience, opinion, perceptions, and perspectives, what do your most challenging figure and God have in common? Journal your response.

Journal

Challenging Relationships

Reflecting on your most challenging relationships, what did / do they have in common with your most challenging parental figure or influential person? Journal your response.

According to your experience, opinion, perceptions, and perspectives, what did / do your most challenging relationships and God have in common? Journal your response.

Journal

Journal

Journal

Journal

Chapter 9

Step 3: Examine Your Thoughts and Feelings

In this next step, you will examine thoughts and feelings that contributed to the creation and perpetuation of your story of your relationship with God. Go within, and be as honest as possible. Journal what comes forward for you as you read through the following ideas. When answering these questions, you can use paper separate from your journal in case you would like to shred these pages after your clearings.

Judgments and Resentments

What judgments / resentments do you hold against your most challenging parent / influential person? Journal your response.

Journal

Journal

Journal

What judgments / resentments do you hold against God? Journal your response.

Journal

What judgments do you hold against yourself as they relate to your relationship with God? Examples: "I am a poor sinner"; "I am lowly and undeserving of God's grace"; and so on. Journal your response.

Relationship "Mirrors" and Projections

Relationships can act as mirrors of both conscious and subconscious feelings, attitudes, beliefs, perceptions, and misperceptions. Quite often, what we do not want to accept in ourselves, we project (or place) onto others—especially things we deem as "negative."

Listed below are additional questions to ask yourself and journal about.

What Do You Not Want to Own About Yourself?

What aspects of your "shadow" side, the part of your personality you judge as "bad," "wrong," and / or "unacceptable," do you perceive?

Journal

What do you hope is not true of your personality—yet most likely is?

What personality characteristics are you most ashamed of?

Ask this next question of someone who knows you well and who you trust to honestly describe your personality. If that is not possible, imagine that someone who knew you well described your personality. What traits did you perceive as "negative" and that trigger a defensive response from you?

What Aspects of Your Personality Do You Embrace?

What do you perceive are aspects of your "positive" side?

What personality characteristics do you most admire in others—and feel are not true of you?

Refer back to how the person you trust described your personality. (Again, if that was not possible, refer back to someone who knew you well and how that person described your personality.) What traits do / did you perceive as "positive" and yet trigger a defensive ("that couldn't possibly be me") response from you?

What Aspects of God's "Personality" Do You Have in Common?

What "personality" characteristics do you think you share with God?

What Is God's True Nature?

What are you hoping is the True Nature of God?

What aspects of God's True Nature do you want to experience, embrace, and embody more of?

Chapter 10

Step 4: Expose Through Divining

In the previous step, you were asked to examine your thoughts and feelings about your perceived relationship with God. Based on what you wrote, you will now be asked to create your own "Lack of Positive" and "Negative / Challenged" statements to use for your "GOD Project." These energetic statements can be used to begin the next step of exposing what needs to be cleared and removed through divining.

Positive and Negative Aspects

As you learned in the main book, I believe a holistic approach to removing blocks and imbalances in the conscious mind and the sub-conscious involves addressing *both* the presence of negative / challenged statement energetics, programs, and vibrations *plus* the lack of positive statement energetics, programs, and vibrations.

Statement Lists Format

The format of the statements lists was designed to support easy tracking of the statements. There is no particular statement hierarchy, order, or grouping. Each chart page has the following:

- Type of Statement (Lack of Positive or Negative / Challenged)
- Page number
- Fifteen statements broken down into three groups (A, B, C) of five statements (1-5) for easy tracking
- A place to note when you were "Challenged" as indicated via divining
    - If test *weak* or *no* regarding a positive statement on a "Lack of Positive Statements" chart

○ If you test *strong* or *yes* regarding a negative statement on a "Negative / Challenged Statements" chart

○ If you test *strong* or *yes* for needing to know more information about the energetic

• A place to notate the energetic was cleared and released

What You Will Be Tracking

During your GOD Project, you will be tracking which energetic statement best represents your "Challenged" energetic blocks and imbalances—and those that are not a challenge *plus* statement energetics what indicate you need to know more information. You will also be tracking the energetic clearing and release.

Challenged Energetics

"Lack of Positive Statements"

○ While divining, if you get a *strong* or *yes* response to a positive statement, you can leave the "Challenged" box clear or mark the box with a "0." (Leaving the box blank makes it easier to clearly spot the checked boxes.) These statements contain the subconscious /unconscious and conscious thoughts, energy, and vibration that resonates as what you hold as *True*.

○ If you get a *weak* or *no* response, mark the *Challenged* box with a "check." These statements represent energetic dissonance and what you hold within your subconscious / unconscious and conscious thoughts, energy, and vibration as *False* or *Not True*.

"Negative / Challenged Statements"

○ While divining, if you get a *weak* or *no* response to a negative statement, mark the box with a "0". These statements contain the subconscious / unconscious and conscious thoughts, energy, and vibration that resonate as what you hold as *False or Not True.*

o If you get a *strong* or *yes* response, mark the *Challenged* box with a "check." These statements contain the subconscious / unconscious and conscious thoughts, energy, and vibration that resonate as what you hold as *True.*

Need to Know More Information (Any Statement)

o While divining, if you get a *strong* or *yes* response after inquiring if you need to know more information, within the *Challenged* box either add an "I," circle the "check," or create your own notation.

Clearing and Releasing

In Chapter 11, you will learn how to clear and release energetic blocks and imbalances.

"Lack of Positive Statements"

o When a "Lack of Positive Statement" energetic clearing and release has taken place, it means that the energetic block and/or imbalance towards resonance with the positive statement and associated energy has been removed.

"Negative / Challenged Statements"

o When a "Negative / Challenged Statements" energetic clearing and release has taken place, it means that whatever negative energetic block and/or imbalance which created resonance with the negative / challenged statement within your subconscious / unconscious and/or energy field has been cleared.

Within the *Cleared* box, you can either write the date it was cleared, check the box indicating a clearing, or write a "C."

In the statements lists in this chapter, the first five pages are blank "Lack of Positive Statements" forms on which you can write your desired positive personal statements. These statements can include what you think, hope, and want to be true of God's nature and your relationship with God—and yet may fear might not be true for you. These pages will also assist you in tracking your progress of clearing and releasing energetic blocks and imbalances that have been separating you from experiencing / perceiving a more loving relationship with God.

NOTE: After your created statements, additional statements are provided.

The lists I have provided regarding both "Lack of Positive Statements" and "Negative / Challenged Statements" are:

- Not all-inclusive
- Not in any specific order or hierarchy
- Merely samplings

NOTE: You might not want to divine each provided energetic statement—or you may want to divine all of them. I suggest that you divine to discern if it would be beneficial for you to use the provided statements—or not.

Following the "Lack of Positive Statements" pages, you will find five blank "Negative / Challenged Statements" forms on which to write your perceived "negative" and/or "challenging" perceptions and feelings statements related to God and your perceived relationship with God. This is where you can track your clearing and releasing of negative perceptions and feelings / energetic blocks and imbalances which have also contributed to your perceived / misperceived separation from God.

Again, after your created statements, additional statements are provided.

NOTE: The number of statements, the exact statements, and the kind of statements ("Lack of Positive" or "Negative / Challenged") that need to be cleared vary for each individual. As more layers are revealed and cleared, even more statements and corresponding energetic vibrations may be revealed. As I wrote in **GETTING GOD™ ~ *"The GOD Project*,"** our perceived challenges can have multiple layers, like an onion, that need to be peeled away one layer at a time.

To get the most transformative value out of this process, it is best to be as vulnerable, open, and honest with yourself as possible. There is no judgment—so go for the greatest amount of healing possible for you at this time.

Remember ...

This is not a mental / thinking / figuring it out process. This is not a processing of any "story" process. It involves trusting what is energetically identified by using energy-identifying tools. If you want to use a mind, allow your God-Mind—your Divine Mind—to lead this process.

Divining Which Statements to Address

Remember to follow all protocols at all times. In this section, you will focus on:

- Following the *Beginning Session Protocol for All Divining Sessions* (see page 66) and
- Following the *Divining Statements Protocol* (see pages 69-70).

Remember—you do not have to divine for each and every statement—or you can. You can begin by addressing the statements you created, or you can begin with the statements provided. There is no *wrong* way to approach this. As always, to find the best way for you to approach these statements, go within, ask, and divine to discern which way would work best for you.

NOTE: Though the statements within the "Lack of Positive Statements" chart are *positive* statements, the intention is to test and track which positive statement energetic is *lacking* or *absent* from one's energy field and/or subconscious.

Lack of Positive Statements (Page 1)	Challenged	Cleared
Group A		
1.		
2.		
3.		
4.		
5.		
Group B		
1.		
2.		
3.		
4.		
5.		
Group C		
1.		
2.		
3.		
4.		
5.		

Lack of Positive Statements (2)	Challenged	Cleared
Group A		
1.		
2.		
3.		
4.		
5.		
Group B		
1.		
2.		
3.		
4.		
5.		
Group C		
1.		
2.		
3.		
4.		
5.		

Lack of Positive Statements (3)	Challenged	Cleared
Group A		
1.		
2.		
3.		
4.		
5.		
Group B		
1.		
2.		
3.		
4.		
5.		
Group C		
1.		
2.		
3.		
4.		
5.		

Lack of Positive Statements (4)	Challenged	Cleared
Group A		
1.		
2.		
3.		
4.		
5.		
Group B		
1.		
2.		
3.		
4.		
5.		
Group C		
1.		
2.		
3.		
4.		
5.		

Lack of Positive Statements (5)	Challenged	Cleared
Group A		
1.		
2.		
3.		
4.		
5.		
Group B		
1.		
2.		
3.		
4.		
5.		
Group C		
1.		
2.		
3.		
4.		
5.		

Lack of Positive Statements (6)	Challenged	Cleared
Group A		
1. God loves me.		
2. God and I are One.		
3. God loves me unconditionally.		
4. God loves me no matter what I say, do, think, or how I behave.		
5. God is loving and kind.		
Group B		
1. My Soul is clean and pure.		
2. God is pleased with me.		
3. God always takes care of me.		
4. God has my back.		
5. God is always with me.		
Group C		
1. God is always there for me.		
2. God accepts me unconditionally.		
3. I don't need to incur God's favor.		
4. God loves and accepts me exactly as I am.		
5. God approves of me.		

Lack of Positive Statements (7)	Challenged	Cleared
Group A		
1. I can trust God.		
2. I trust God		
3. It is safe for me to trust God.		
4. I am capable of sensing God's loving presence in my life.		
5. God wants a close relationship with me.		
Group B		
1. Prayers work.		
2. My prayers work.		
3. God listens to me and my prayers.		
4. I am capable of loving God.		
5. I love God.		
Group C		
1. God holds nothing against me.		
2. God forgives me.		
3. God always forgives me.		
4. God forgives me even before I ask for forgiveness		
5. I am forgiven.		

Lack of Positive Statements (8)	Challenged	Cleared
Group A		
1. It is easy for me to approach God.		
2. I am a beloved child of God.		
3. God cares about me and embraces who I am.		
4. I don't need to prove anything to God.		
5. I am worthy of God's Love.		
Group B		
1. I am worthy of God's forgiveness.		
2. I am worthy in God's eyes.		
3. I am worthy.		
4. I am a beautiful, pure, and clean Soul in God's eyes.		
5. My Soul is whole and holy.		
Group C		
1. Hearing the word "God," I feel _____ (inner peace, pure Love, connection, joy).		
2. God withholds nothing from me.		
3. It is God's great joy, happiness, and pleasure to "give me God's Kingdom."		
4. When I think of God, I think of pure Love and acceptance.		
5. God is not responsible for _____ (whatever grievance comes to mind).		

Lack of Positive Statements (9)	Challenged	Cleared
Group A		
1. I am capable, open, and willing to have a close relationship with God.		
2. I have a close relationship with God.		
3. I am a beloved child of God, in whom God is well pleased.		
4. God is pure Love.		
5. As pure Love, God is incapable of holding grudges.		
Group B		
1. As pure Love, God's Love does not have to be earned.		
2. As pure Love, it is impossible for God to abandon me.		
3. I am connected to God.		
4. As pure Love, it is impossible for God to separate from me.		
5. As pure Love, God is only capable of loving me.		
Group C		
1. God is pure acceptance.		
2. I do not have to be perfect to be loved and accepted by God.		
3. As pure Love and pure acceptance, God loves and accepts me.		
4. I am capable of accepting that God loves and accepts me—exactly as I am.		
5. I accept God's Love for me and God's acceptance of me.		

Lack of Positive Statements (10)	Challenged	Cleared
Group A		
1. As pure Love, God is always there for me.		
2. Even if I do not call on God, as pure Love, God is always there for me.		
3. God supports me.		
4. I feel that God supports me.		
5. I believe that God supports me.		
Group B		
1. I don't need to do anything to deserve God's Love.		
2. I don't need to do anything to deserve God's grace.		
3. I don't need to do anything to deserve God's mercy.		
4. I don't need to do anything to deserve God's forgiveness.		
5. As pure Love and acceptance, I do not need to do anything for God's Love and acceptance.		
Group C		
1. God is not the cause of suffering.		
2. As pure Love and acceptance, God does not judge me.		
3. As pure Love and acceptance, God does not test me.		
4. God provides me with opportunities to learn lessons, grow, and evolve.		
5. Everyone has her or his own path of growth, learning, and spiritual evolution.		

Lack of Positive Statements (11)	Challenged	Cleared
Group A		
1. As pure Love, God would never and could never forsake or abandon me.		
2. God cares about the world.		
3. I always know I am connected with God—no matter what.		
4. God's Heart is open to me.		
5. I am open and receptive to God's Heart.		
Group B		
1. I am capable of experiencing God.		
2. I am open and receptive to experiencing God.		
3. God is here for me.		
4. God exists in my life.		
5. I am in partnership with God.		
Group C		
1. Nothing separates me from God.		
2. Nothing separates me from God's Love.		
3. I feel close to God.		
4. I feel loved by God.		
5. I feel safe with God.		

Lack of Positive Statements (12)	Challenged	Cleared
Group A		
1. God cares for and about me.		
2. There is no separation between me and God.		
3. I don't need to do anything to prove my love to God.		
4. I don't need to do anything to earn God's Love.		
5. God's Love doesn't need to be earned.		
Group B		
1. I don't need to do anything before making a conscious connection with God.		
2. Consciously aware of it or not, I am always connected with God.		
3. Miracles can happen in my life.		
4. If there is a heaven, God wants me there and will allow me in.		
5. I am more than good enough for God.		
Group C		
1. I talk with God and God listens.		
2. I am capable of receiving messages from God.		
3. I am open and receptive to receiving messages from God.		
4. As pure Love and acceptance, God does not measure my faith.		
5. No matter what I say or do, I will never be unworthy in the eyes of God.		

Lack of Positive Statements (13)	Challenged	Cleared
Group A		
1. My relationship with God is a source of joy, loving, comfort, acceptance, and support.		
2. My relationship with God is a two-way street— God to me and me to God.		
3 My relationship with God is comfortable and easy.		
4. My relationship with God is important to me.		
5. I am important to God.		
Group B		
1. In God's eyes, I am a delight.		
2. I know God.		
3. I am pleasing to God.		
4. God know, loves, accepts, and approves of me.		
5. I am important to God, and my relationship with God is important to me.		
Group C		
1. I feel safe in my relationship with God.		
2. As pure Love and acceptance, God would not and could not ever turn against me.		
3. Because God is pure Love and acceptance, I feel safe and comfortable with God.		
4. As pure Love and acceptance, God's loving presence is always with me.		
5. I am safe and secure in God's Love.		

Lack of Positive Statements (14)	Challenged	Cleared
Group A		
1. I don't have to beg and plead with God to forgive me.		
2. God is not mad at me.		
3 As pure Love and acceptance, God is not capable of being mad at me.		
4. God is not waiting to smite me.		
5. God is my divine supporter.		
Group B		
1. I am open to miracles in my life.		
2. I am receptive to miracles in my life.		
3. I believe miracles can happen in my life.		
4. I witness the miraculous in everyday living.		
5. God is in partnership with me		
Group C		
1. I understand the true meaning of surrender.		
2. I am capable of surrendering to God and God's will.		
3. I am willing to surrender to God and God's will.		
4. I feel safe surrendering to God and God's will.		
5. I surrender to God and God's Will.		

Lack of Positive Statements (15)	Challenged	Cleared
Group A		
1. I can easily make a conscious connection with God.		
2. I know how to open my heart to God.		
3. I am capable of opening my heart to God.		
4. I am willing to open my heart to God.		
5. I open my heart to God.		
Group B		
1. I am not angry with God.		
2. I am not separate from God.		
3. I am glad to consciously connect with God.		
4. My love for God is unconditional.		
5. I don't judge God.		
Group C		
1. I feel connected with God		
2. My connection with God is a source of joy and delight.		
3. My connection with God is a source of love, support, and acceptance.		
4. I feel my connection with God is strong.		
5. God is with me and inside of me.		

Lack of Positive Statements (16)	Challenged	Cleared
Group A		
1. God does not want me to suffer.		
2. God does not require me to suffer.		
3. I do not have to atone for my sins through pain and suffering.		
4. God does not demand pain and suffering.		
5. God does not demand that I experience pain and suffering.		
Group B		
1. I want to open my heart to God.		
2. My heart can open to God.		
3. I don't need to do anything to incur God's favor.		
4. There is connection between the Heart of God and my heart.		
5. My heart is open.		
Group C		
1. God is real for me.		
2. I am beloved by God.		
3. It is safe for me to open my heart to God.		
4. If there is a heaven, I am worthy of going there.		
5. It is safe for me to surrender to God and God's will.		

Lack of Positive Statements (17)	Challenged	Cleared
Group A		
1. God cares about me.		
2. I know how to love God.		
3. God is there for me and supports me.		
4. I am capable of having an experience of God's Love for me.		
5. I please God.		
Group B		
1. It is safe for me to love God unconditionally.		
2. God's Love is real for me.		
3 I am a Divine Being experiencing a human incarnation.		
4. My Soul is open to God.		
5. God has forgiven me.		
Group C		
1. I am capable of hearing and knowing God's promptings.		
2. No matter what I have done, God is ready, willing, and able to forgive me.		
3. When I talk to God, God hears me.		
4. I am able to discern God's voice from my ego's voice.		
5. God is my beloved.		

Negative / Challenged Statements

If during divining of the *Negative / Challenged Statements*, you test *strong* or *yes* for a statement, check the "Challenged" box. These statements contain energetic / vibrational blocks, imbalances within your subconscious / unconscious—and perhaps even within your conscious awareness—that would be beneficial for you to clear and release to be less encumbered by negativity toward yourself and toward your perceived relationship with God.

If you are prompted to divine for more information and/or if there is an indication that the energetic represented within the statement was inherited, make sure to notate it.

While divining, if you get a *weak* or *no* response to the "Negative / Challenged" statement, you can leave the "Challenged" box clear or mark the box with a "0." (Leaving the box blank makes it easier to spot the checked boxes.) These statements contain the subconscious / unconscious and conscious thoughts, energy, and vibration that resonate as what you hold as *False* or *Not True*.

After doing the clearing and release work, within the *Cleared* box you can either write the date it was cleared, check the box indicating a clearing, or write a "C."

Negative / Challenged Statements (Page 1)	Challenged	Cleared
Group A		
1.		
2.		
3.		
4.		
5.		
Group B		
1.		
2.		
3.		
4.		
5.		
Group C		
1.		
2.		
3.		
4.		
5.		

Negative / Challenged Statements (2)	Challenged	Cleared
Group A		
1.		
2.		
3.		
4.		
5.		
Group B		
1.		
2.		
3.		
4.		
5.		
Group C		
1.		
2.		
3.		
4.		
5.		

Negative / Challenged Statements (3)	Challenged	Cleared
Group A		
1.		
2.		
3.		
4.		
5.		
Group B		
1.		
2.		
3.		
4.		
5.		
Group C		
1.		
2.		
3.		
4.		
5.		

Negative / Challenged Statements (4)	Challenged	Cleared
Group A		
1.		
2.		
3.		
4.		
5.		
Group B		
1.		
2.		
3.		
4.		
5.		
Group C		
1.		
2.		
3.		
4.		
5.		

Negative / Challenged Statements (5)	Challenged	Cleared
Group A		
1.		
2.		
3.		
4.		
5.		
Group B		
1.		
2.		
3.		
4.		
5.		
Group C		
1.		
2.		
3.		
4.		
5.		

Negative / Challenged Statements (6)	Challenged	Cleared
Group A		
1. God is angry with me.		
2. God wants to punish me.		
3. God scares me.		
4. God is mean.		
5. God is going to send me to Hell.		
Group B		
1. I am a poor sinner, and God hates sinners.		
2. God hates me.		
3. God is illusive.		
4. God wants me to suffer.		
5. God is vindictive and spiteful.		
Group C		
1. God does not love me.		
2. God's acceptance of me is conditional.		
3. God's Love is conditional.		
4. God is always testing me.		
5. I am always failing God's tests.		

Negative / Challenged Statements (7)	Challenged	Cleared
Group A		
1. I can't trust God.		
2. I don't trust God.		
3. I won't trust God.		
4. I don't know how to trust God.		
5. I am afraid to trust God.		
Group B		
1. Prayers don't work.		
2. My prayers don't work.		
3. God ignores me and my prayers.		
4. I talk to God, but God ignores me.		
5. I must incur God's favor for God to respond to me.		
Group C		
1. No matter what I do, I cannot incur God's favor.		
2. God does not forgive me.		
3. God will not forgive me.		
4. I am unforgivable.		
5. I am an abomination in God's eyes.		

Negative / Challenged Statements (8)	Challenged	Cleared
Group A		
1. God does not approve of me.		
2. God does not approve of what I do.		
3. God is ashamed of me.		
4. I am ashamed and unworthy of God's Love.		
5. I am ashamed and abandoned by God.		
Group B		
1. I am not worthy of God's forgiveness.		
2. I am not worthy of God's Love.		
3. I am not worthy.		
4. I am not worthy in God's eyes.		
5. I must prove to God that I am worthy.		
Group C		
1. Even hearing the word "God," I feel _____.		
2. God withholds things from me (money, loving relationships).		
3. God withholds good things from me.		
4. God withholds _____ from me.		
5. I cannot forgive God for _____.		

Negative / Challenged Statements (9)	Challenged	Cleared
Group A		
1. I will never figure God out.		
2. I will never have a close relationship with God.		
3. God takes pleasure in my suffering.		
4. It is holy to be punished.		
5. God holds grudges.		
Group B		
1. I must earn God's Love.		
2. I will never earn God's Love.		
3. I am separate and apart from God.		
4. I am not able to connect with God.		
5. God has abandoned me.		
Group C		
1. I must be perfect in order for God to love me.		
2. I am not perfect so God will never love me.		
3. I will never be acceptable to God.		
4. I cannot accept that God loves me.		
5. I cannot accept God's Love for me.		

Negative / Challenged Statements (10)	Challenged	Cleared
Group A		
1. God is mercurial—supposed to be loving, but in a flash, God is angry and mean.		
2. When I needed God the most, God abandoned me.		
3. I don't believe God supports me.		
4. I don't feel that God supports me.		
5. I don't believe that God wants to support me.		
Group B		
1. I don't deserve God's love.		
2. I don't deserve God's grace.		
3. I don't deserve God's mercy.		
4. I don't deserve God's forgiveness.		
5. I don't deserve God.		
Group C		
1. God demands that I suffer.		
2. I am angry with God for allowing bad things to happen to me.		
3. I am angry with God for allowing bad things to happen to my family / those I love.		
4. I am angry with God for allowing bad things to happen.		
5. I am angry with God.		

Negative / Challenged Statements (11)	Challenged	Cleared
Group A		
1. If there was a God, then _____ should have never happened.		
2. If God loved me, God would make me whole / healthy. (God doesn't love me—or God _____.)		
3. If there was a God, God would heal _____.		
4. If there was a God, God wouldn't allow _____ to suffer.		
5. If there was a God, God would not allow so much suffering.		
Group B		
1. I don't know how to experience God.		
2. I don't know what to do to be able to experience God's Love.		
3. God isn't there.		
4. God isn't there for me.		
5. God does not exist for me.		
Group C		
1. There is an impermeable wall that separates me from God.		
2. There is an impermeable wall that separates me from God's Love.		
3. I have feelings of resentment toward God.		
4. I feel lost and unloved by God.		
5. I feel forsaken by God.		

Negative / Challenged Statements (12)	Challenged	Cleared
Group A		
1. God just doesn't care about me.		
2. God just doesn't care about the world.		
3. God is too demanding.		
4. I don't know what God demands of me.		
5. I will never be able to achieve all that God demands of me.		
Group B		
1. I am a sinful wretch.		
2. My Soul is unclean.		
3. No matter how good I am, I will never be good enough for God.		
4. If there is a heaven, I will never be able to enter.		
5. Living on Earth is a punishment from God.		
Group C		
1. It is bad and wrong to question God.		
2. It is bad and wrong to question my religion.		
3. My faith is not strong enough for God.		
4. I must do penance before I can approach God.		
5. No matter what I say or do, I will never be worthy in the eyes of God.		

Negative / Challenged Statements (13)	Challenged	Cleared
Group A		
1. My relationship with God is frustrating.		
2. My relationship with God is a one-way street—me to God.		
3. I have tried so hard with God, so trying again, or more, seems pointless and useless.		
4. Getting my relationship with God straightened out is useless.		
5. I am doomed ... so what's the point?		
Group B		
1. Try as I might, I will always fall short in God's eyes.		
2. Only good and holy people get to know God.		
3. I have to be holy to please God.		
4. I am not holy enough to please God.		
5. I will never be good or holy enough to please God.		
Group C		
1. I do not feel safe in my relationship with God.		
2. God will turn on me.		
3. God could turn on me any second—and that scares me.		
4. God is unpredictable.		
5. My position with God is uncertain.		

Negative / Challenged Statements (14)	Challenged	Cleared
Group A		
1. I have to beg and plead with God to forgive me.		
2. Even if I plead for forgiveness, God may not forgive me.		
3. Even if I plead for forgiveness, God will not forgive me.		
4. What I have done is unforgiveable.		
5. God will never forgive me.		
Group B		
1. I am not capable of being forgiven.		
2. God's heart is closed to me.		
3. God doesn't care for me or about me.		
4. I need to prove my love to God.		
5. I need to prove my love to God, but I don't know how to do that.		
Group C		
1. I am not open to miracles in my life.		
2. I am not receptive to miracles in my life.		
3. I don't believe miracles can happen in my life.		
4. Miracles will never happen for me.		
5. Miracles only happen to good people—like saints.		

Negative / Challenged Statements (15)	Challenged	Cleared
Group A		
1. Surrendering to God and God's will is not safe.		
2. Surrendering to God is scary.		
3. I am afraid to surrender to God and God's will.		
4. I am not willing to surrender to God and God's will.		
5. I don't know what it means to surrender.		
Group B		
1. I fear God—and God scares me.		
2. I can't find God.		
3. I don't know how to get close to God.		
4. I don't know how to open my heart to God.		
5. My heart is closed to God.		
Group C		
1. I am mad and angry at myself for not being able to connect with God.		
2. I am sad that I cannot connect with God.		
3. I feel lost and confused without a connection with God.		
4. My love for God is conditional.		
5. I judge God as wrong / bad / uncaring / unloving / not there / not there for me / _____.		

Negative / Challenged Statements (16)	Challenged	Cleared
Group A		
1. God doesn't want to give me "The / God's Kingdom."		
2. God is depriving me of "The / God's Kingdom."		
3. I have to walk on eggshells with God.		
4. I love God but God doesn't seem to love me.		
5. God is punishing me.		
Group B		
1. God is not inside of / within me.		
2. There is no forgiveness for me and what for what I have done.		
3. I must suffer for God.		
4. God requires me to suffer.		
5. I must suffer to be considered holy and righteous.		
Group C		
1. I need to atone for my sins through pain and suffering.		
2. The only way I can atone for my sins is through pain and suffering.		
3. Penance for my sins requires pain and suffering.		
4. I must prove to God that I am sorry for my sins by experiencing pain and suffering.		
5. God demands pain and suffering.		

Negative / Challenged Statements (17)	Challenged	Cleared
Group A		
1. Something is wrong with me that I can't connect with God.		
2. I am not enough for God.		
3. My heart is closed.		
4. God is illusive to me.		
5. God doesn't think I am worthy.		
Group B		
1. God demands suffering from me.		
2. I am closed to God.		
3. I avoid God because God scares me.		
4. I need to prove something to God but I don't know what.		
5. I don't know how to love God the way God wants me to.		
Group C		
1. If I surrender to God, I will die.		
2. I judge God as being _____.		
3. I am afraid to surrender to God.		
4. I am afraid to get close to God.		
5. If there is a heaven, God will never allow me to enter.		

Negative / Challenged Statements (18)	Challenged	Cleared
Group A		
1. No matter what I do, I will never be good enough for God.		
2. I am being punished by God.		
3. I don't know how to love God.		
4. God doesn't care about me.		
5. It is useless for me to approach God.		
Group B		
1. Regarding God, I am a poor victim.		
2. God turns on people / God turns (turned) on me.		
3. If there was a God, God wouldn't be so distant.		
4. I don't know where I stand with God.		
5. I can't experience God.		
Group C		
1. I am eternally damned.		
2. God has forsaken me.		
3. If God loved me, God would not be punishing me.		
4. God does not exist.		
5. I don't please God.		

Chapter 11

Step 5: Eliminate Through Energetic Clearing and Releasing

Over the years I have studied numerous subconscious / unconscious emotional and energetic clearing and releasing modalities. I have even become certified in various clearing and releasing modalities. Additionally, I have been inspired to create additional techniques and protocols.

I am sharing two modalities with you in this chapter. The first is what I call the **Brow, Crown, and Down** method; the second I call the **Acu-Points Rub / Tap** method. Neither is superior to the other; they are just two that worked for me. As a first step, you must discern which modality to use.

NOTE: During any energy clearing and releasing session, you may experience some emotional energy releases (tears, crying, laughing) plus other energetic releases (deep sighing, yawning) during the clearing and release process. If this should happen, it simply means that e-motion (energy in motion) is occurring. During my own "GOD Project," I experienced dream-like images, intuitive impressions, felt the energy of certain emotions, experienced sound and colors, and received inner messages. If you do not experience a noticeable emotional release or any of what I described that I experienced, it does not mean that a clearing and release did not occur. You can always verify a clearing through divining.

Divining Which Clearing Modality to Use Protocol

- Use divining to discern which clearing and releasing modality would be best for you to use at this time.

- ***Brow, Crown, and Down***? (Y/N?)
- ***Acu-Points Rub / Tap***? (Y/N?)

NOTE: If you test *no* (*weak*) for both, discern which other modality to use (for example, one you may be familiar with and have experience with) by using your intuition and divining.

- Discerning suggestions:
  - ○ Connect within. Ask for clarity and guidance regarding which modality to use at this time.
  - ○ After receiving the indication of which modality to use at this time, ask:
    - ▪ *Is it safe and supportive for me to continue at this time?* Divine.
- If *yes*, continue. If you get a *no*—stop!
- Refer to ***What to Do If You Get a No (Weak) to Proceed*** on pages 68-69.

Brow, Crown, and Down Method

Both your fingertips and a magnet emit and carry electromagnetic energy, so your tools consist of:

- Your fingertips
- Optional: magnet (This can be a refrigerator magnet.)

Energy Clearing and Release Protocol for All Sessions

- Follow the ***Beginning Session Protocol for All Divining Sessions***.
- Follow ***Divining Statements Protocol***.
- Follow ***Divining for More Information Protocol***.
- Follow ***Divining Which Clearing Modality to Use Protocol***.
- If the ***Brow, Crown, and Down*** method is indicated, proceed.

Energetic Clearing and Release Procedures for "Negative / Challenged Statements"[8]

This is the procedure to use if, when divining, you test *strong* (*yes*) regarding a "Negative / Challenged" statement and are guided to use the **Brow, Crown, and Down** method. (This indicates there is resonance between you and the negative / challenged energetic.)

- Using your fingertip(s), begin by either lightly rubbing in a circle (for a few seconds—approximately 5-6 small circles) or tapping (approximately 5-6 times) on the area of your brow / third eye (area between eyebrows and at the center of the forehead). Proceed rubbing or tapping at various spots along the meridian line up to your crown (top of the head) and down (the back of your head to behind your neck). Rub or tap along the path described.

- Modifications:
  - Sweep your fingertips instead of tapping. Sweep several times. (I tend to sweep five or six times.)
  - Sweep the magnet instead of rubbing or tapping. Sweep several times.
  - At the same time, state (verbally or silently) one or more of the following statements:
    - "Release. Release. Release."
    - "Be gone. Be gone. Be gone."
    - "I AM releasing blocks now."
    - "I Am free! I Am free! I Am free!"
    - Or create something to that effect.

NOTE: For me, most of the time I would lightly rub about 3-6 circles or tap 3-6 times per point along the meridian path (or 3-6 fingertip /

---

[8] If the statement energetic is inherited, refer to **Clearing and Releasing Inherited Energy Protocol for All Statements (Brow, Crown, and Down Method)** on p. 182.

magnet swipes along the meridian path); other times it would take more than six. When uncertain, I would divine to discern how many circular rubs / taps / swipes would be best. It may vary from time to time. Follow your intuition.

If you are uncertain about any element, divine within yourself. Ask how many times to rub, tap, or sweep to permanently clear and release the energy. After practicing these techniques, you can learn to know, intuitively, how many times to use to rub, tap, or sweep with your fingertips or magnet along the **Brow, Crown, and Down** meridian.

Clearing and Releasing Inherited Energy Protocol for All Sessions (Brow, Crown, and Down Method)

If there was an indication for you to divine for more information and there was an indication that the energy / vibration was inherited,

- Send a blessing to your ancestor while simultaneously:
  - Doing more **Brow, Crown, and Down** rubs / taps / sweeps—more times than you usually would—and the amount you are intuitively guided to do and/or the amount you discern via divining.
  - Additionally, rub or tap more places along the meridian path.
  - Visualize a cord being untied, a chain broken, a lock opening between you and your ancestor as it relates to that specific statement, or whatever else comes forward for you.
  - You can also state things like:
    - "Release and go in peace."
    - "I honor and bless you. Be at peace. Now release."
    - Or whatever you feel your intuition is guiding you to state.

Confirm the Clearing and Release

- Ask: *Has this been released?* Divine.

- If you get a strong (*yes*) response, confirm the release.

How to Confirm the Release of a "Negative / Challenged Statement" Energetic

- Say the statement (either verbally or silently) and then divine again.

- You should test *weak* (*no*).

- If you test *weak* (*no*) to the "Negative / Challenged" statement,

   - Ask: *Is it safe and supportive for me to continue at this time?* Divine.

   - If you get a *strong* (*yes*) response, continue.

NOTE: If you still get a *strong* (*yes*) response to the "Negative / Challenged" statement—stop!

   - Ask: *Is it safe and supportive for me to continue at this time?* Divine.

   - If you get a *strong* (*yes*) response,

      - Restate your intention to release the "Negative / Challenged" energetic.

      - Rub, tap, or sweep more times.

         ▲ Remember: If this was an inherited energetic, the clearing and releasing will require more rubs / taps / swipes.

         ▲ Say the statement (either verbally or silently) and then divine again.

            ◊ You should test *weak* (*no*).

ANOTHER NOTE: If you still test *strong* (*yes*) for the "Negative / Challenged" statement energetic or get a *weak* (*no*) response after asking if it is safe and supportive to continue at this time, follow the same protocols explained in **What to Do If You Get a No (Weak) to Proceed** on pages 68-69.

Energetic Clearing and Release Procedures for "Lack of Positive Statements"[9]

This is the procedure to use if, when divining, you test *weak (no)* regarding a "positive" statement using the **Brow, Crown, and Down Method**. (This indicates there is dissonance / non-resonance between you and the positive energetic.)

- While rubbing or tapping each meridian point, or swiping along the meridian pathway, you can say (either verbally or silently)—following your Intuition / Inner Guidance regarding which statement to say, when to say it, and so on—one or all of the following statements:

    o "It safe for me to experience _____."
    Example: "It is safe for me to experience God's Love of me."

    o "I welcome the energy of _____ now."
    Example: "I welcome the energy of God's Love for me now."

    o "It is for my maximum benefit to accept and experience _____ now."
    Example: "It is for my maximum benefit to accept and experience God's Love for me now."

    o And/or whatever else you feel, intuitively, to state ...

- Also, you can specifically address the blocks and/or imbalances:

---

[9] If the statement energetic is inherited, refer to **Clearing and Releasing Inherited Energy Protocol for All Statements (Brow, Crown, and Down Method)** on pp. 182-183.

- ○ "It is safe for me to remove all blocks and imbalances toward experiencing _____ now."
- ○ And / or something similar. Follow your intuition.

Confirm the Clearing and Release Protocol

- Ask: *Has this been released?* Divine.
- If you get a strong (*yes*) response, confirm the release.

How to Confirm the Release of a "Lack of Positive" Statement Energetic

- Say the statement (either verbally or silently) and then divine again.
- You should test *strong* (*yes*) for the "positive" statement energetic.
- If you test *strong* (*yes*) to the statement,
   - ○ Ask: *Is it safe and supportive for me to continue at this time?* Divine.
   - ○ If you get a *strong* (*yes*) response, continue.

NOTE: If you still get a *weak* (*no*) response to the "positive" statement—stop!

   - ○ Ask: *Is it safe and supportive for me to continue at this time?* Divine.
   - ○ If you get a *yes* (*strong*) response,
      - ▪ Restate your intention to release the "Lack of Positive" energetic.
      - ▪ Remember: If the statement's energetic / vibration is inherited, refer to **Clearing and Releasing Inherited Energy Protocol for All Statements (Brow, Crown, and Down Method)**, see pages 182-183.

- Say the statement (either verbally or silently) and then divine again.

- You should test *strong* (*yes*) response.

ANOTHER NOTE: If you still test *weak* (*no*) for the "positive" statement energetic or get a *weak* (*no*) response after asking if it is safe and supportive to continue at this time, refer to **What to Do If You Get a No (Weak) to Proceed** on pages 68-69.

Always remember: Be gentle with yourself. Drink lots of water. Try again another day.

Acu-Points Rub / Tap Method

Below are the procedures I follow when I use the **Acu-Points Rub / Tap Method.**

Tools:

- Fingertips

- Awareness of some meridian acu-points: (partial listing)

  - top of the head / crown

  - "third eye" area / top of brow (center forehead above eyebrows)

  - side of the eye / temple

  - under the eye

  - under the nose / above the lip

  - under the ear

  - middle of chin

  - below collar bone / below where the collarbone sticks out

  - front side of arm pits

  - sides of rib cage

      o side of palm (below index finger)

      o web between index finger and thumb

      o hugging the wrist with opposite hand

NOTE: Again, not all of these points need to be rubbed in a circular motion or tapped. Additionally, other points can be rubbed or tapped. Some systems use more, some use less.

If this technique is new to you, I suggest you first practice rubbing or tapping on all of the points listed. I tend to rub or tap the following: crown, brow area, side of the eye, under the eye, under the nose / above the lip, middle of chin, below collar bone, side of palm, index / thumb web (sometimes), as well as hugging the wrist of one hand with the other hand. Sometimes I rub or tap additional areas; sometimes I rub or tap very few areas.

Energy Clearing and Release Protocol for All Sessions

- Follow the **Beginning Session Protocol for All Divining Sessions.**

- Follow **Divining Statements Protocol.**

- Follow **Divining for More Information Protocol.**

- Follow **Divining Which Clearing Modality to Use Protocol.**

- If the **Acu-Points Rub / Tap Method** is indicated, proceed.

Energetic Clearing and Release Procedures for "Negative / Challenged Statements"[10]

This is the procedure to use if you, when divining, test strong (yes) regarding a "negative" or "challenged" statement—indicating a resonance between you and the negative / challenged energetic—and guided to use the **Acu-Points Rub / Tap Method.**

---

[10] If the statement energetic is inherited, refer to **Clearing and Releasing Inherited Energy Protocol for All Statements (Acu-Points Rub / Tap Method)** on pp. 188-189.

- Using your fingertips, begin lightly rubbing or tapping (5-6 circular rubs or taps ... or as many times as you are intuitively directed to rub or tap, or however long it takes for you to complete one of the statements below) on the meridian points suggested or indicated.

- While rubbing or tapping on each point, say (verbally or silently)—following your Intuition / Inner Guidance regarding which statement to say, when to say it, and so on—one or all of the following statements:

  o "Release. Release. Release."

  o "I release this energy from me now."

  o "Time to let this go."

  o "It is for my highest good to release this now."

  o "It is safe for me to let this go now."

  o "I Am ready, willing, and able to let go of this now."

  o Or say whatever else you feel, intuitively, you want to state.

Clearing and Releasing Inherited Energy Protocol (Acu-Rub / Tap Method)

If there was an indication for you to divine for more information and there was an indication that the energy / vibration was inherited,

- Send a blessing to your ancestor while simultaneously doing more acu-point rubs / taps—more times than you usually would—and the amount you are intuitively guided to do and/ or the amount you discern via divining.

- Additionally, rub or tap more acu-points along the meridian path.

- Visualize a cord being untied, a chain broken, a lock opening between you and your ancestor as it relates to that specific statement, or whatever else comes forward for you.

  o You can also state things like:

- "Release and go in peace."

- "I honor and bless you. Be at peace. Now release."

- Or whatever you feel your intuition is guiding you to state.

Confirm the Clearing and Release

- Refer to *How to Confirm the Release of a "Negative / Challenged Statement" Energetic* (pages 183-184).

Energetic Clearing and Release Procedures for "Lack of Positive Statements"[11]

This is the procedure to use if, when divining, you test *weak (no)* regarding a "positive" statement using the *Acu-Points Rub / Tap* method. (This indicates there is resonance between you and the negative / challenged energetic.)

- While rubbing or tapping on each meridian point, you can say (either verbally or silently and following your Intuition / Inner Guidance concerning which statement to say and when to say it—or something similar) one or all of the following statements:

    o "It safe for me to experience _____."
    Example: "It is safe for me to experience God's Love of me."

    o "I welcome the energy of _____ now."
    Example: "I welcome the energy of God's Love for me now."

    o "It is time for me to experience _____ now." Example: "It is time for me to experience God's Love for me now."

    o "It is for my maximum benefit to accept and experience _____ now."
    Example: "It is for my maximum benefit to accept and experience God's Love for me now."

---

[11] If the statement energetic is inherited, refer to *Clearing and Releasing Inherited Energy Protocol for All Statements (Acu-Points Rub / Tap Method)* on pp. 188-189.

- o "I Am ready, willing, and able to embrace _____ now."
  Example: "I Am ready, willing, and able to embrace God's Love for me now."

  o And/or whatever else you feel, intuitively, to state …

- Also, you can specifically address the blocks and/or imbalances:

  o "It is safe for me to remove all energetic blocks and imbalances toward experiencing _____ now."

  o "I Am ready, willing, and able to clear and release any and all blocks toward _____ now."

  o "It is time to let go of all blocks and imbalances preventing me from experiencing _____ now."

  o And / or something similar. Follow your intuition.

Confirm the Clearing and Release

- Refer to *How to Confirm the Release of a "Lack of Positive Statement" Energetic* (see pages 185-186).

Other Energetic Clearing Modalities and Sources of Information

As mentioned several times, there may be another / other clearing and releasing modality / modalities you may be directed to use. You may also be directed to change the healing modality to use for each clearing session. As always, use your Intuition / Inner Guidance and divine to discern which energetic clearing and release modality would be most beneficial at the time and each time you do this work.

Again—and as always—other sources of information are going within, directly asking God / Spirit / Highest Power, and using your intuition. Ask for guidance and support. Affirm clarity.

BOTTOM LINE: Go within. Meditate. Breathe. Be still. Be open. Be flexible. Connect with your Intuition and Inner Guidance—the Divine Within.

Additional Support

Journaling is a useful way to express and explore your thoughts, feelings, experiences, and insights. It is also a wonderful way to document and track your progress.

Journal Your Session Experiences

In your journal, make notes regarding the experience of your session— both during and immediately after each session. Sometimes, while doing this type of work, you receive epiphanies, inspirations, revelations, images, and / or messages. Document these, as they may provide material to further explore in subsequent meditations, and this information can be used to create intentions, affirmations, and so on.

Journal Your Dreams

Additional information may also be revealed during your dream state. Always keep a journal and pen near your pillow or bedside. Grab them prior to or as soon as you open your eyes, and begin writing whatever you can gather and/or recall. (Opening the eyes for too long before writing can result in losing the message, as another type of processing of sensory information kicks in.) Do not worry about your handwriting or your spacing on the page. Write key words, impressions, phrases, descriptive images—anything and everything you can possibly recall. These notations can also be explored in more depth in your meditations and used to inform your intentions, affirmations, and prayers.

Chapter 12

STEP 6: EMPOWER

At this point in your "GOD Project," I want to offer suggestions to support you in positively reinforcing and shoring up any and all new and "positive" perspectives regarding God / Spirit / Highest Power and your perceived relationship with God. Below are all things I have used and have found to be successful for reinforcing lessons learned, insights gleaned, and relationship "improvements" (on my part).

Revisit and Review

After being vulnerable and putting heart-centered time, energy, and focus on your transformation, I believe it is good to positively reinforce and support such work. One way to do this is by reviewing your tracking notes. Notice any improvements?

Journal about your observations of the review of your tracking.

Journal

Journal

Journal

Another way to support yourself is to review your progress. Retake the Stress / Challenge Evaluation. (See page 79.)

Journal about any changes you noted between your "before" and "after" Stress / Challenge Evaluation.

Journal

Journal about how you perceive God and your relationship with
God now. *How do you feel? What do you think?*

Journal

Journal

Additionally, journal what you are grateful for. (You can also make a list starting with the words "I Am grateful for ...") state gratitude for anything and everything—including what you learned as a result of doing your "GOD Project"—and your gratitude for what you have learned about you, God, and/or your perceived relationship with God.

Journal

Journal

Journal

Continuing Supportive "GOD Project" Relationship Practices

Maintaining a positive relationship—with anyone—requires time, energy, effort, positive focus, commitment, devotion, communication, and honesty—just to name a few key elements. The same is true as it relates to improving your perceived relationship with God.

Here are some ways I have incorporated these elements:

- Meditating—listening to God.

    ○ I set the intention to meditate at least two or three times a week between 10 and 20 minutes per session. I schedule that time on my calendar and do it while seated in a chair with good back support.

- Tracking

    ○ Track delightful synchronicities—what I call "God winks"

    ○ Times I felt I experienced God's presence

    ○ Times I experienced God through others

    ○ Times I experienced God's love, grace, and so on

- Journaling

    ○ Writing about what I was tracking and my tracking experience

    ○ Writing / expressing my thoughts, feelings, ideas, and gratitude

    ○ Documenting my session experiences, dreams, impressions, messages, and revelations

    NOTE: I am not a very consistent journal writer. I do, however, experience value when I actually do journal.

- Checking within—connecting with myself; connecting with Spirit; connecting with Spirit and myself—as a whole

    ○ I do this several times a day. I used to have an application on my computer that could be programmed to "chime" at desired intervals. When I heard the chime (approximately every two hours from 9:00 a.m. to 5:00 p.m.), I would stop what I was doing, stretch, take a few deep breaths, say a favorite mantra, say a prayer, or simply say, "Hi God! It's me, Linda!" Then I would stretch again, and resume what I was doing.

- Writing positive affirmations
  - I always enjoy this activity. I invite my playful inner child to assist me with creating positive affirmations.
- Setting positive intentions upon waking regarding my perceived relationship with God
  - Upon waking and prior to opening my eyes, I ask myself a version of these questions:
    - *What do I want to be today?* (Joyful? Playful? Productive? Loving? Supportive?)
    - *What do I want to experience today?* (Love? Joy? Productivity? Inspiration? Creativity? Playfulness?)
    - *God, what would you like me to experience today?*
    - *God, what would you like me to learn today?*
    - *God, what would you want me to embody today?*
- Upon waking, expressing gratitude
  - Express gratitude (silently, verbally, and/or via journaling) for anything and everything.
    - I begin with the statement *"I Am grateful for ..."* and then state whatever comes forward.
- Prior to sleeping, expressing gratitude
  - Express gratitude (silently, verbally, and/or via journaling) for anything and everything.
    - You can begin with the statement *"I Am grateful for ..."* and then state whatever comes forward.
- Also prior to sleeping, setting my intentions to use this time to enable my subconscious mind to relax during my sleep

time and to enable blocks and/or imbalances to be cleared and released in an easy and gentle manner—and to wake refreshed and invigorated. Prior to being a student at USM, I sporadically set intentions before going to sleep. While a student, this became a nightly practice. It has now become a supportive habit.

- ○ First, I thank God for the day.

- ○ Next, I say a prayer and then set my intentions of effortless clearing, releasing, and healing while my body experiences reparative and restorative sleep.

- ○ I set my intention to awake refreshed, replenished, and renewed.

- Socializing with energetically and spiritually uplifting people.

- ○ This is such a fun and supportive step. I love having conversations that matter with members of my spiritual "tribe"—"my peeps." I enjoy being silly and playful with them too.

- Being of service to others

- ○ Every time I volunteer, I set a service intention. Offering selfless service in support of others is a wonderful way to practice connecting with God in a conscious way. It is also a wonderful way to consciously practice seeing and connecting to God's Spirit within others.

- ○ I view serving others as an opportunity to practice being God's hands and feet and God's Mind and Heart.

- Getting additional support on all levels. Some examples:

- ○ Spiritual: seeking spiritual counseling, prayer support

- ○ Some churches offer supportive spiritual counseling, prayer services, and prayer support. I know of a church that has a prayer "hotline." I sometimes ask my friends for "Love and Light" support—and I provide the same for them. I am on several prayer lists. I also fill out a "Request for Prayer Support" if the church I am visiting offers one.

If candles are offered, I also light a candle while stating my prayer and / or intention.

- Seeking additional energetic healing. I love learning about healing modalities. I love that I can find a myriad of Spirit-connected and Spirit-gifted facilitators of healing. In addition to being blessed to have studied and become certified in various healing modalities myself, I love experiencing the gifts of clearings, releasing, healing, and upliftment facilitated by others.

Regardless of your religion or denomination, here are some additional things you can do to support yourself in connecting to God Within and God Throughout:

- Chant, recite mantras
    - I use what I have learned from various spiritual venues—that resonate within and invoke a more positive, uplifted, and open state within me.
    - I also enjoy creating my own chants and mantras.
- Sing or listen to spiritually uplifting songs
    - My "go-to" playlist is Christmas music—regardless of what season of the year it is! Gospel music also inspires and delights me.
    - I also enjoy writing my own lyrics to songs. I get the karaoke versions of certain songs and enjoy singing the new lyrics I create for them.
- Listen to spiritually based inspirational and uplifting recordings
    - I love listening to audio recordings of certain spiritually based books, workshops, and talks.
- Read spiritually oriented books and articles
    - I started re-reading the New Testament and focused on what Jesus said.

- ○ I read and practice "Lessons" from *A Course in Miracles*.

  ○ I enjoy reading and / or listening to life stories and teachings of great spiritually enlightened way-showers.

- Attend spiritually based inspirational and uplifting workshops, seminars, and training programs

  ○ I enjoy attending workshops given by my favorite transformation-oriented and spiritually oriented authors. It gives me an opportunity to incorporate what they have written about on another level—in a more interactive way and with a community of fellow seekers.

  ○ I took classes at a local church that I resonated with.

  ○ I take spiritually oriented online classes and workshops.

- Attend spiritually inspirational services and celebrations

  ○ At times, I attend church services offered by my religion of origin. Sometimes hearing and singing some of my favorite inspirational songs from when I was a child gives me joy and some comfort because of my familiarity with the music. Other times, I attend a church or service that I am not familiar with to explore, learn, and grow. Either way, I enjoy the sense of community—a gathering of Souls longing to connect with their Highest Power.

- Ask questions and seek answers

  ○ I go within and ask God for answers and insights regarding my questions, confusion, concerns—about anything and everything. After following the standard protocol that I shared with you prior to beginning each and every clearing session, I visualize myself standing before God and asking questions. Now that I have become more comfortable with this process, I actually visualize myself sitting in front of God—and having an actual dialogue.

Remember ...

> Ask and it will be given to you; seek and you will find; knock and the door will be opened to you.(7)

> For everyone who asks receives; the one who seeks finds; and to the one who knocks, the door will be opened.(8) (Matthew 7:7-8, NIV)

Chapter 13

Moving Forward

Change can be quite threatening to some people. Any change.

After releasing old and ineffective energy blocks and imbalances (both conscious and unconscious / subconscious) and incorporating new insights and ways of being within yourself (toward God, others, and to life and living in general), moving forward is the next step.

Moving forward takes courage. That is especially true when unhappy, angry, fearful, and judgmental people notice a shift in you. Some may feel threatened because your reaction to the interaction between the two of you is no longer the same or predictable. Your responses and interactions become unpredictable—and this can be quite unsettling for them. Some may want to remind you of your past in an attempt to keep you bound, captive, held hostage, and forever tethered to your past. They want to define you based on their perceptions / misperceptions of their—and your—past. They view you through their rearview mirror.

Actually, all this does is keep *them* tethered to *their* own past— *their* own misperceptions and distortions based on *their* own inner negativity. They are trying to hoist their negative perceptions of their past into their—and your—present and future. These people want to hold on to their own past and use it as a weapon to keep you in place. That "place" happens to be within their own negativity, judgments, unhappiness, and fear. They think they can use that "place" as leverage to control you. In fact, it only serves as a means of constriction and confinement within them. It holds *them* hostage and bound to *their* past.

Others, who have not yet moved forward themselves, may say things such as:

- "How dare you rock the boat!"
- "I remember when you said (or did) _____."
- "You acted like _____."
- "I remember the time when you were _____."
- "I will never forget the time when you said (or did) _____."
- "I will never forgive you for _____."
- "I will never forget or forgive you for the time when you _____."

Energetic Qualities of Moving Forward

- Having determination / resolve
- Embracing fortitude / perseverance
- Loving and caring for everyone involved, including yourself
- Releasing
- Allowing
- Being nonjudgmental

Examples of Moving Forward

When confronted and challenged by those in fear, resistance, and judgment who are experiencing anger, unhappiness, and discontent within their own lives, it would behoove you to focus your energy and attention on your continuing transformation. Focus on your intentions and commitment to your growth and upliftment. In other words, "Keep on keeping on."

A more positive reframing or perceiving of others' reactive and negative responses to your evolution can be applied to the degree of others' reactions (such as anger, disturbance, reactiveness, defensiveness, and attacking). Neutrally observing the amount and / or intensity of others' negative reactions can be a great tool for you to measure how much you have grown, been uplifted, and transformed. More simply stated, the strength of others' negative reactions can reflect, proportionally, the degree to which you have transformed.

Some things to consider: Sometimes "allowing" and "releasing" may mean allowing other people to be themselves and releasing any and all judgments you may have against *them* for how they are reacting to your transformation. At times, it may mean releasing the relationship—allowing your continuing upliftment and transformation with freedom from their negative reactions, energy, repercussions, and interference.

BOTTOM LINE: At all times, try your utmost to be loving and caring toward everyone—especially those who are on a different path in life. May *everything* serve as a blessing and lesson for you. Again, at all times, try your utmost to be grateful for the gifts and blessings that negatively reactive people have been in your life, and bless them and their journeys through life. Move forward on your own path—loving them *and* yourself—along the way.

Questions and Responses

Question: How do I refer to exact statement numbers? Is this correct: Negative / Challenged Statement, Page #3, Group C, Statement #4?

Response: Keep things simple and easy. You can create a way of documenting that works for you. This is how I do it: using the same statement above, I document it as: –3C4; a "Lack of Positive Statement": +3C4.

Q: Can any of the *challenges* be inherited?

R: Yes. You can inherit a lot from your ancestors—including lines of energy. It is possible that you can inherit negative lines of energy from your ancestors on either side of your family regarding both the presence of negative / challenged energy and the lack of positive energy. (**NOTE:** It is also possible to have inherited "positive" lines of energy too!)

Q: How will I know if these *challenges* were inherited or not?

R: You can always ask by going within and divining for the answer. Most likely, if you need to know additional information (for example, maternal or paternal side; male or female relative), it will be indicated with a *strong* or *yes* response at the time you ask whether or not you need to know additional information. If you do get a *strong* or *yes* response, you can discern through divining:

- *"Was this issue inherited?"* (Yes/No)

If you continue to get a *yes* response, you can continue to discern through divining:

- *"Maternal side?"* (Y/N)
- *"Paternal side?"* (Y/N)

After this, continue to ask if you need to know additional information or not.

If you get a *weak* or *no* response, you do not need to know additional information. I suggest you simply move on.

Q: If something is found to be inherited, does that mean a direct bloodline kind of thing?

R: Yes and no.

- Yes: Just as one inherits DNA from one's ancestors / lineage, so can one inherit a line of energy.

- No: While you may not have inherited a challenge via your ancestor's / lineages' direct bloodline, you can still "take on" a group's / family's line of energy. For example, if you join or expand into a "new family" by way of marrying into another family or becoming part of a blended family—or change religions—you become immersed in the energetic line of that family's / tribe's / religious group's belief system. That energetic line may be taken on—embraced, so to speak. It can permeate and / or hover within and around your energy field. This means you can "inherit" (or "take on") an energy line of a belief system that you were not born into—without a direct physical, bloodline inheritance.

NOTE: Even within a family / "tribe" / religion, not everyone deals with the same "inherited" energetic—or energetic statement. Even identical twins may not have the same "inherited" energetic blocks and imbalances. The reasons for this phenomenon are varied: lessons to be learned, one's individual Soul's path, and so on. Different people and different belief systems refer to this individualization by different terms: one's lot in life, fate, lessons, karma, and so on.

Another way of viewing the concept of an "inherited" energetic is this: Some people believe that the Soul continually evolves and does so by reincarnating and experiencing many different lifetimes. Again, believing in or not believing in reincarnation is *not* part of this program. I am simply sharing a perspective.

If, however, you do believe in reincarnation, a way of explaining individualization and inheritance of energetic lines of energy is as follows: A *challenged* line of energy can be "inherited" / carried over from one lifetime to another—until it is finally cleared and released.

Q: If there is a statement with a blank to fill in (for example, –3C4: "God withholds _____ from me"), what do I do if I have a list with more than one item?

R: Take a moment, go within, and see what comes forward. You might only have one issue come up. If, however, you get a list of things, ask yourself and discern through divining:

- *"Do I have to clear each issue individually?"* (Y/N)

If you get a *yes*, make a list of each issue, write a statement, and energetically clear and release each statement individually.

If, however, you get a *no*, you can confirm this by asking:

- *"Can I clear everything all together?"* (Y/N)

You should get a *yes*.

Q: I divined and got the exact same statement to clear twice. What's up with that?

R: You most likely forgot to check (the first time) whether or not you needed to know more information about the energy surrounding the statement. As an example, if the energy was "inherited," you need to do more circular rubs or taps, swipes of your fingers or magnet, or more light rubbing on the points along the **Brow, Crown, and Down** meridian pathway again.

Next steps:

- Discern if you need to know any more information.
- If you divine a *yes*, clear again.
- Make sure you do additional circular rubbing, tapping, or sweeps of your fingertips or magnet, or lightly rub the meridian points again, as indicated through divining / your intuition.

If, after following the protocol above, you still get the same statement to clear, it may be that there is a similar energetic that is close to, but not the specific or exact word / emotion / energy / vibration presently within the statement, that still needs to be cleared.

219

After you clear that original statement,

- Go within and ask what the energetic is it that needs / wants to be cleared,

- Follow your intuition, and then ...

- After you receive a sense of what that energetic may be, discern through divining:

  - *"Is* (substitute the new word / emotion / energetic in that same statement) *the energetic that needs to be cleared?"* (Y/N)

What comes forward for you, after going within and following your intuition, is most likely what was trying to get your attention by making you go back and revisit a particular statement. On numerous occasions, that is what I experienced.

NOTE: Words are limiting. Sometimes, while some words' energetic vibrations are close or similar, they are not the exact vibration that needs to be released. Another possibility is that some energetic vibrations may have needed to be cleared and released *prior* to the exact energetic vibration being able to come to the fore to be cleared and released. Additionally, this could also be a practical example of the "gatekeepers" at work.

BOTTOM LINE: This is a process. Always be gentle and patient with yourself and your own process as you gently remove various energetic layers to access the core / root of the energetic to clear and release it.

Q: Through divining, I was directed to clear something that I did not test for as something that needed to be addressed. Why?

R: Sometimes, after there has been clearing and releasing of some energy statements' vibrations, other energetic statements—that formerly tested one way—may change. There is a reason for this.

Healing can be described as the unpeeling of a multi-layered onion or the removing of the prickly leaves of an artichoke to ultimately reveal the heart inside. Somewhat similar to the answer to the previous question about clearing the same statement twice, once one layer is cleared and released it may create a cleared space that allows for the other energetic vibration / energy statement to come forward to be cleared and released next. While this may not happen often, it can happen.

Suggestion: After you have completed all of your clearings, go to each statement page ("Lack of Positive" and "Negative / Challenged" statements). Go within and ask:

- *"Have all the statements that need clearing and releasing on this page been cleared and released?"* (Y/N)

    o If you get a *yes*, all is complete.

    o If you get a *no*, divine which statement(s) need to be cleared and released, and then proceed to clear and release them.

    o Discern, via divining, which needs to be cleared first ... next ... next ...

Q: What did you experience during your clearing and release sessions?

R: There were times when I was excited to do this work. Other times I felt extreme resistance. Sometimes within the same session, I would experience both. Quite often, it seemed like I was on a roller-coaster ride.

Sometimes, just the revealing of the energy statement to work on stirred emotions and energy within. One of my session journal entries reads:

Just upon discovering this was the one [statement] to be worked on, I cried. The energetic of the revealing of this statement was just so intense ... overwhelming ... sad? I did not even have time to mentally process or contemplate the statement's words or meaning. I had a spontaneous outburst of energy—tears. It was somewhat an experience of relief in just the discovery and uncovering of the entrenched [negative] energetic vibration. The emotion did not come from me thinking about the statement—its meaning or implication. My emotion simply arose upon the discovery and revealing of a deeply hidden and embedded energetic block and bringing the block into the Light. Tears of joy, perhaps ...

Q: What did you experience after your sessions?

R: Sometimes I felt sleepy and would take a nap. Other times, I felt lighter—more buoyant energy compared to the denser energy I felt prior to the start of the session. Other times, I felt nothing.

It is important to note that using emotions as a gauge of clearing and releasing is *not* reliable. Always discern, via divining, that a clearing and release has taken place. If you get a *yes*, accept it. Own it. Embrace it. Move on.

Q: What did you do to prepare for your sessions?

R: I did some prep work on all levels.

- Environmentally: I made sure that the space in which I was doing my session was comfortable and quiet and that I would not be disturbed by others. I also made sure that my phone was off.

- Physically: I drank lots of water prior to and after all sessions.

- Mentally: I set intentions.

- Emotionally: I checked my attitude to make sure I was open and receptive to transformation and not disturbed, distracted, preoccupied, or upset by something.

- Spiritually: Sometimes I meditated. Most times, I said a prayer.

Q: What has changed, if anything, as a result of you doing your "GOD Project"?

R: Tons. Within my inner environment, I have experienced greater:

- Inner peace

- Trust in God / the Universe—that the best and greatest of everything will happen for myself and others

- Comfort by releasing the erroneous notion that I can "control" anything

- Sense of being in the flow—not having to plan, alter, or maneuver anything

- Acceptance and allowance—releasing the need to harshly judge myself and others

- Forgiveness—releasing my past and the past of others

- Letting go and releasing my perceived "mistakes" / "errors" / "sins" / misperception positions that I have held against myself

- Letting go and releasing the "mistakes" / "errors" / "sins" / misperceptions of others that I have held against them

- Conscious awareness of my ever-present connection with my Inner Guidance / Intuition / Inner Knowing—aspects of God Within—and with God Throughout

- Conscious awareness that God communicated and continues to communicate with me in a myriad of ways including via Inner Guidance / Intuition / Inner Knowing

- Conscious connection to the present—here and now

- Relaxation because I do not have to "figure things out" on any and all levels and in all departments of my life: financial, career, relationships, and so on

- Relief that I do not have to "process" anything—which only keeps me in my head and stuck within the mental level

- Calmness because there is significantly less inner chatter from my "monkey / munching mind"

- Deeper breathing and the experience of a greater sense of "safety"—knowing that I do not have to "walk on eggshells" with God

- Compassion, for myself and others, and empathy—knowing that we each did the very best we knew how to do given what we knew at each and every stage in our lives

- Confidence—knowing that God has my back

- Assuredness—knowing I am a beloved child of God

- Loving—toward God, myself, and others

Just to name a few benefits that come to mind ...

Q: Any other advice or suggestions you can offer?

R: Be gentle with yourself.

- Take a nap if you need one.

- Shower or take a bath after a clearing and release session if that supports you.

- Stop effort-ing, angst-ing, analyzing, figuring things out, processing, over-processing, perpetuating stories, creating stories, being harsh with yourself and your path—and the path of others.

- Remember: This is not a monkey-mind / figuring-out / mental processing task.

- Allow and accept what was and what is—and move on.

- Embrace and own your good and the good of God.

- Let love and the vibration of loving be your guide in all things.

- When you want to know something, go within—and ask God to reveal God's Truth to you.

- Ask God to reveal God's True Nature to you.

- Remember—If you allow it to be so, you will be guided and supported in this process. God is on your side ... and so am I.

If you are interested in booking private support sessions, visit www.DrLindaHumphreys.com.

Summary of Divining Steps
and
Energy Clearing and Releasing Protocols

Below you will find a list of steps and protocols that can assist you with the divining process and with the energetic clearing and releasing during your "GOD Project."

- Beginning Session Protocol for All Divining Sessions (p. 66)
- Establish Your Baselines (All Divining Sessions) (p. 67)
  - What to Do If You Are Not Able to Discern Your Yes and No (pp. 67-68)
- Divining Continuation Protocol (p. 68)
  - What to Do If You Get a No (Weak) to Proceed (p. 68)
- Divining Statements Protocol (pp. 69-70)
  - Divining for More Information Protocol (pp. 71-72)
- Divining Which Clearing Modality to Use (pp. 179-180)
- Energy Clearing and Release Protocol for All Sessions (p. 180)
- Energetic Clearing and Release Procedures for "Negative / Challenged" Statements
  - Brow, Crown and Down Method (pp. 181-182)
  - Acu-Points Rub / Tap Method (pp. 187-188)
- Confirm the Energetic Clearing and Release (p. 183)
- How to Confirm the Release of a "Negative / Challenged Statement" Energetic (pp. 183-184)
  - Brow, Crown and Down Method (pp. 183-184)
  - Acu-Points Rub / Tap Method (same as Method above)
- Clearing and Releasing Inherited Energy Protocol for All Statements (p. 182-183)
  - Brow, Crown and Down Method (pp. 182-183)
  - Acu-Points Rub / Tap Method (pp. 188-189)
- Confirm the Clearing and Release (p. 183)

- Brow, Crown and Down Method (pp. 183-184)
- Acu-Points Rub / Tap Method (same as Method above)

- Energetic Clearing and Release Procedures for "Lack of Positive Statements" Energetic
  - Brow, Crown and Down (pp. 184-185)
  - Acu-Points Rub / Tap Method (pp. 189-190)

- Confirm the Energetic Clearing and Release (p. 185)

- How to Confirm the Release of a "Lack of Positive Statement" (pp. 185-186)
  - Brow, Crown and Down (pp. 184-185)
  - Acu-Points Rub / Tap Method (p. 189-190)

- Clearing and Releasing Inherited Energy Protocol for All Statements
  - Brow, Crown and Down Method (pp. 182-183)
  - Acu-Points Rub / Tap Method (pp. 188-189)

- Confirm the Clearing and Release
  - Brow, Crown and Down (pp. 185-186)
  - Acu-Points Rub / Tap Method (pp. 185-186)

References

Airodyssey.net. "Inflight Passenger Announcements." Accessed March 7, 2017.

https://airodyssey.net/reference/inflight

American Airlines. "Airline Safety Video," YouTube Video, 4:20, September 22, 2016.

www.youtube.com/watch?v=LXb28mVZiJo

Bibleinfo.com. "What Are the Seven Deadly Sins?" Bible Questions. Accessed March 2, 2017.

www.bibleinfo.com

Brennan, Barbara Ann. *Hands of Light: A Guide to Healing through the Human Energy Field*. New York: Bantam Books, 1988.

Chakras.info. "The 7 Chakras." Accessed February 7, 2017.

www.chakras.info

DeMille, Cecil, dir. *The Ten Commandments*. 1956. Hollywood: Paramount, 1999. DVD.

Dispenza, Joe. *Breaking the Habit of Being Yourself: How to Lose Your Mind and Create a New One*. San Diego: Hay House, 2012. Kindle edition.

Edwards, Jonathan, and Smolinski, Reiner, ed. "Sinners in the Hands of an Angry God. A Sermon Preached at Enfield, July 8th, 1741." Sermon, Enfield, 1741. Electronic Texts in American Studies, 54. *http://digitalcommons.unl.etas/54*

Erickson, Alexa. "20 Quotes by Rumi that Will Make You Feel the Love." *Collective Evolution*. Last modified October 29, 2013. *www.collective-evolution.com*

Goodreads.com. "Quotes." Last accessed November 14, 2016.

www.goodreads.com.

Hawkins, David R. *Power vs. Force: The Hidden Determinants of Human Behavior, Author's Official Revised Edition*. San Diego: Hay House, 2012. Kindle edition.

Heriot, Drew, dir. *The Secret*. 2006. Australia, Primetime Productions, 2006. DVD.

The Holy Bible: King James Version. Accessed Nov 14, 2016. http://biblehub.com

Horan, Ellamay, and Newton, Wm. L. *The Illustrated Revised Edition of Baltimore Catechism No. 1*. New York: W.H. Sadler, Inc., 1944.

Jung, C. G. *Dreams*. Translated by R.F.C. Hull. Princeton: Princeton University Press, 1974.

Kelley, Bennet. *Saint Joseph First Communion Catechism*. New York: Catholic Book Publishing Co., 1963.

King James Bible with VerseSearch: Red Letter Edition (Kindle Locations 39277-39280). Seattle: Amazon Digital Services LLC: 2013. Kindle edition.

Lamsa, George M. *Holy Bible: From the Ancient Eastern Text*. New York: HarperCollins, 1933. Kindle edition.

Luton, Frith. "Carl Jung Projections." Frithluton.com. Accessed March 2, 2017.
http://frithluton.com

Martino, Joe. "20 Profound Quotes by Carl Jung that Will Help You to Better Understand Yourself." *Collective Evolution*. Last modified January 25, 2016.
www.collective-evolution.com

Mollon, Phil. "Thought Field Therapy and its Derivatives: Rapid Relief of Mental Health Problems through Tapping on the Body." *Primary Care and Community Psychiatry* 12, no. 3-4 (December 2007): 2-6. doi: 10.1080/17468840701750836.

Newton, John. *Amazing Grace*. Timeless Truths Free Online Library. Accessed March 3, 2017.

http://library.timelesstruths.org

"Quotes of Michelangelo." Michelangelo Paintings, Sculptures, Biography. Accessed March 3, 2017.

www.michelangelo.org

Shen-Nong Limited. "Meridians." Shen-Nong.com. Accessed February 27, 2017.

www.shen-nong.com

"Sin." Wikipedia. Accessed July 31, 2018.

https://en.wikipedia.org/wiki/Sin

Sister Annunziata. *Sister Annunziata's First Communion Catechism*. New York: Benziger Brothers, Inc., 1946.

"Socrates Quotes." BrainyQuote. Accessed March 1, 2017. www.brainyquote.com.

"The Structure and Function of a Healthy Spine: Cleveland Clinic." Accessed February 27, 2017.

https://my.clevelandclinic.org

Tompkins, Peter, and Bird, Christopher. *The Secret Life of Plants*. New York: Harper & Row Publishers, Inc., 1973.

Walsch, Neal Donald. *Conversations with God: Book I*. Charlottesville, Virginia: Hampton Roads Publishing Company, Inc., 2012.

Williamson, Marianne. *A Return to Love: Reflections on the Principles of A Course in Miracles*. New York: Harper Collins, 1992.

Acknowledgments

Thank you
God / Spirit / My Higher Power—without whom I could not do anything.
I am in awe, deeply humbled and grateful for
the miraculous positive transformations in my life.

To my teachers and "way-show-ers":
Dr. Seuss (aka: Theodore Seuss Geisel)
The Pathwork
Dr. Carl Rogers
Dr. Carl Jung
Marianne Williamson
A Course in Miracles
Rev. Dr. Michael Beckwith
Dr. Paul Barrett
Conversations with God
Drs. Ron and Mary Hulnick
Dr. Caroline Myss
Dr. Joe Dispenza
Dr. Robert Holden

To my dear friends, who made me laugh—especially at myself.

To my "spiritual friends"—
my "nudge-rs" / prodders / stackers / "thorns in my side"
through whom I have learned some of my greatest spiritual lessons
along the way.
Y'all know who you are. ☺

To Jeff—
a source of an abundance of great love,
joy, fun, adventure, laughter, and support.

And, as always...
Thank you, BABY JESUS!!!
Amen.

About the Author

I am a seeker.

I am a perpetual student.

I make mistakes.

As a seeker and student, I have learned from my mistakes and am now making conscious strides to "choose again," as *A Course in Miracles* suggests.

I believe in releasing any / all perceived internal confines (judgments, misperceptions)—especially related to the past.

I believe in all forms of forgiveness—including self-forgiveness.

I believe in learning lessons, releasing the past—and moving on.

I believe in being grounded in the present moment because this is where the magic happens. I strive to be present—to fully show up and be "all in"—in all I do.

I believe in being more loving and compassionate toward myself and others in the present—which sets the tone for a more love-filled present—and paves the way for a more love-filled future.

I made a commitment to transform—on all levels.

I strive for personal excellence.

I believe in change, transformation, miracles, and the power of Love.

I view my transformed life as a miracle.

I made a commitment to support others in their transformation and support them in experiencing their own miracles.

My zodiac sign is Gemini.

My "birth card" is Ace of Clubs.

My Enneagram test revealed that I have many personality tendencies (with "tied" scores in both my number one and two positions) with lotsa "wings" to support me.

I don't expect other people to "figure me out" because I can't "figure" myself out.

I tell those I love to "strap on your seat belt" and enjoy the ride when they are with me.

I love flowers.

Tulips make me smile.

I love the scent of carnations.

Laughter makes me laugh.

I love to laugh.

I love spending time with friends.

I believe in "retail therapy."

I love new adventures.

I love delightful surprises.

I love traveling and meeting new people.

I love 70 percent dark chocolate, Utz potato chips, and eating
Maryland crab ... anything.

I love to eat.

I love my various families, tribes, and peeps.

I love my husband.

I love America.

I love the entire Universe.

I love children.

I love God.

I love "Baby Jesus."

I love you.

Linda Humphreys, PhD
www.DrLindaHumphreys.com

Real joy comes when we get the right desire met—the desire for God, for a life led by the Spirit, fulfilling not our material desires but our deepest need, which is to be in a close relationship with our Creator. That is the source of true blessing. The only source.

— Michael W. Smith